Levers of Control

Levers of Control

How Managers Use Innovative Control Systems to Drive Strategic Renewal

Robert Simons
Harvard Business School

Harvard Business School Press
Boston, Massachusetts

Library of Congress Cataloging-in-Publication Data
Simons, Robert.
    Levers of control : how managers use innovative control systems to drive
strategic renewal / Robert Simons.
      p.   cm.
    Includes bibliographical references and index.
    ISBN 0-87584-559-2 (alk. paper)
    1. Industrial management.   2. Strategic planning.
3. Controllership.   I. Title.
HD31.S563   1994
658.4'012—dc20   94-9073
                                                                      CIP

Contents

Preface   ix

Part I   Strategy, Organizations, and Control   1

  1. Introduction   3
    • Control and Control Systems in Organizations   5
    • Controlling Business Strategy   8
    • Organization of the Book   10

  2. A Balancing Act: Tensions to Be Managed   13
    • The Dynamics of Creating Value   14
    • The Dynamics of Strategy Making   18
    • The Dynamics of Human Motives   21
    • The Dynamics of Controlling Business Strategy   28
    • Summary   29

Part II   Basic Levers of Control   31

  3. Beliefs and Boundaries: Framing the Strategic
    Domain   33
    • Beliefs Systems   33
    • Boundary Systems   39
    • Actions Speak Louder than Words   55
    • Beliefs, Boundaries, and Managers   55
    • Beliefs, Boundaries, and Control Staff Specialists 56
    • Summary   57

v

4. Diagnostic Control Systems: Implementing
   Intended Strategies   59
   • Alternatives to Diagnostic Control   61
   • Intended Strategy and Critical Performance
     Variables   63
   • Conserving Management Attention   70
   • Design Considerations   71
   • The Role for Staff Groups   85
   • Asset Acquisition Systems as Diagnostic Control
     Systems   87
   • Summary   89

5. Interactive Control Systems: Adapting to
   Competitive Environments   91
   • Strategic Uncertainties   93
   • Interactive Control Systems   95
   • Linking the Concept of Interactive Control
     Systems to Other Theory   103
   • Design Considerations   108
   • Roles for Managers and Staff Groups   121
   • Summary   123

Part III A Dynamic Framework for Controlling Business
          Strategy   125

6. The Control Levers in Action   127
   • How Ten New Senior Managers Use the Levers
     of Control   129
   • Cluster 1: Strategic Turnaround   131
   • Cluster 2: Strategic Evolution   141
   • Relative Success   147
   • Analysis of the Managers' Actions   148
   • Summary   151

7. The Dynamics of Controlling Business Strategy   153
   • Using the Control Levers to Guide Strategy   153
   • Balancing Empowerment and Control   162
   • Implications for Managers   166
   • Summary   175

Appendix A   Checklist Summary of the Levers of Control   177

    • Lever #1: Beliefs Systems   178
    • Lever #2: Boundary Systems   178
    • Lever #3: Diagnostic Control Systems   179
    • Lever #4: Interactive Control Systems   180
    • Foundation: Internal Control Systems   181

Appendix B   Use and Misuse of Information Technology   183

    • Levers of Control and Information Technology   186

    References   197

    Index   209

Preface

I began work on this book more than ten years ago with a simple question: How do managers balance innovation and control? Data that I had collected from over one hundred companies revealed a puzzling anomaly: the most innovative companies used their profit planning and control systems more intensively than did their less innovative counterparts. I had expected the opposite result. Existing theory predicted that innovative companies should minimize formal controls to reduce bureaucracy and allow creativity to flourish.

Since then, I have studied scores of highly regarded companies and the control levers their senior managers use. In my teaching at Harvard, I have developed case studies in a variety of industries and have refined concepts with both executives and MBA students. A number of organizations have successfully implemented these ideas. The product of this work is an action-oriented theory of control that is, I hope, both cohesive and comprehensive.

The management literature provides little systematic guidance for controlling strategy, especially in organizations that demand innovation and flexibility. We know much about techniques for analyzing markets and formulating winning strategies. But the best-laid plans are worthless if they cannot be implemented successfully. This book attempts to bridge the gap by describing new concepts and tools that successful managers use to transform the tension between creative innovation and predictable goal achievement into profitable growth.

This book will be of interest to several audiences: general managers concerned with executing strategy; staff professionals who design and implement systems for performance measurement and control; and students of management—academics and consultants—seeking to develop theories of managerial action. It draws upon accounting and control to reveal the power of goal setting and performance measurement, strategic management to understand the process by which strategy is formulated and implemented, and business policy for an appreciation of the adminstrative and leadership challenges that confront senior managers.

Leveraging opportunity and attention is at the heart of the analysis. This is no accident. Two remarkable universities—McGill and Harvard—have helped shape my beliefs about how focused knowledge, coupled with commitment, can unleash the potential of emerging opportunities. My doctoral thesis at McGill's Faculty of Management set me on a course that has been rewarding beyond my expectations. Haim Falk and Henry Mintzberg gave me the tools and the inspiration to set out on a path of discovery. With Haim and Henry as role models, I have never doubted the rewards—both personal and professional—of the journey.

Harvard Business School is a special place that still awes me with its uncompromising mission and unparalleled intellectual resources. I owe a great debt to many colleagues who have helped me here, especially Dean John McArthur, whose untiring efforts created the unique environment of which I am a beneficiary. Two people in particular have served as a daily reminder of what makes Harvard unique. Bob Kaplan has been a source of intellectual strength and encouragement. As a colleague and friend, Bob demonstrates a rare combination of rigor and open-mindedness that revels in identifying important problems and searching for new understanding. Warren McFarlan, through his personal energy and interest, has marshalled the institutional resources to support my research and teaching. Equally important, Warren proved a valued colleague and counsel as I made the research and teaching decisions that would ultimately shape the ideas set forth in this book.

Special thanks go also to Chris Argyris, who has shown unflagging interest in helping me piece together the arguments in a coherent and rigorous way, and to Hilary Weston, who worked with me during one (all too short) year in developing teaching materials to bring these concepts to life in the classroom. Others who have taken time from busy schedules to work through ideas with me include Joe Bower,

Bill Bruns, Robert Burgelman, Chuck Christenson, David Collis, Dwight Crane, Marc Epstein, Thérèse Flaherty, Jay Lorsch, Jim McKenney, Denise Nitterhouse, Krishna Palepu, Tom Piper, Richard Rosenbloom, Bill Rotch, Dan Schendel, Howard Stevenson, John Vogel, and John Waterhouse.

Doctoral students have the undistinguished honor of being captive audiences for the emerging, unpolished ideas of their professors. As scholars in training, these students' enthusiasm and willingness to test ideas are important stimuli for the development and refinement of new theory. Several doctoral students have, with characteristic good humor, contributed critiques and suggestions that have improved my work, notably Alan Branson, Scott Camlin, Tony Davila, Dale Geiger, Scott Keating, Kentaro Koga, Jean-François Manzoni, Sarah Mavrinac, Charlie Osborn, and Sarah Tasker.

I am indebted to all of the MBA students, executive program participants, and senior managers who knowingly and unknowingly helped me develop the theories and action principles outlined in this book. Underestimating the importance of their ideas and feedback would be a serious mistake. Pauline Henault and Beverly Outram provided invaluable secretarial support for my various research and teaching projects. The staff at Baker Library were also enormously helpful through the various stages of the work. Finally, Carol Franco, senior editor at Harvard Business School Press; Barbara Roth, managing editor; and Patricia Carda, copy editor, provided the encouragement and skill to transform a rough manuscript into the book that you hold in your hands.

This book is dedicated to my parents, Joan and Les, and to my wife and soulmate, Judy, who has shared with me the successes and setbacks along the way.

Cohasset, Massachusetts

Strategy, Organizations, and Control

CHAPTER 1

Introduction

This book provides a new, comprehensive theory for controlling business strategy. Over the past two decades, management theorists and economists have devoted a great deal of energy to understanding strategy formation in competitive markets. They have developed techniques for analyzing the relative economic advantage of differentiated product and service offerings, but they have paid relatively little attention to understanding how to implement and control strategies. Yet the best-laid plans are worthless unless business managers understand the tools and techniques of strategy implementation.

Notwithstanding recent advances in theories of organization and strategy, the tenor of management control reaches back to the 1960s. A "command-and-control" rhetoric underlies phrases associated with traditional management control: top-down strategy setting, standardization and efficiency, results according to plan, no surprises, keeping things on track.

But command-and-control techniques no longer suffice in competitive environments where creativity and employee initiative are critical to business success. Increasing competition, rapidly changing products and markets, new organizational forms, and the importance of knowledge as a competitive asset have created a new emphasis that is reflected in such phrases as market-driven strategy, customization, continuous improvement, meeting customer needs, and empowerment.

The tension between the old and the new reflects a deeper tension between basic philosophies of control and management:

Old	New
Top-down Strategy	Customer/Market-Driven Strategy
Standardization	Customization
According to Plan	Continuous Innovation
Keeping Things on Track	Meeting Customer Needs
No Surprises	Empowerment

How can organizations that desire continuous innovation and market-driven strategies use management controls that are designed to ensure no surprises? How can empowerment and customization be reconciled with management controls that seek to standardize and ensure that outcomes are according to plan?

In searching for answers to these questions, we cannot dismiss too quickly traditional means of control. We can ask just as easily how empowered organizations guard against flawed decisions by subordinates who may not share the same goals or information as senior management, or how far-flung, complex businesses achieve constancy of purpose if continuous innovation results in needless experimentation and conflicting initiatives.

Understanding how to control empowered organizations in highly competitive markets is important for both theorists and practicing managers. My colleague Michael Jensen concluded his 1993 presidential address to the American Finance Association with this enjoinder, "Making the internal control systems of corporations work is the major challenge facing economists and management scholars in the 1990s" (Jensen 1993).

A new theory of control that recognizes the need to balance competing demands is required. Inherent tensions must be controlled, tensions between freedom and constraint, between empowerment and accountability, between top-down direction and bottom-up creativity, between experimentation and efficiency. These tensions are not managed by choosing, for example, empowerment over accountability—increasingly, managers must have both in their organizations.

This book presents a comprehensive theory illustrating how managers control strategy using four basic levers: beliefs systems, boundary systems, diagnostic control systems, and interactive control systems. The solution to balancing the above tensions lies not only in the technical design of these systems but, more important, in an understanding of how effective managers use these systems. The four control levers are nested—they work simultaneously but for different purposes. Their collective power lies in the tension generated by each lever.

Control and Control Systems in Organizations

Control in organizations is achieved in many ways, ranging from direct surveillance to feedback systems to social and cultural controls. Rathe noted some fifty-seven connotations of the term *control* (1960, 32). Clearly, terminology can cause confusion if not defined precisely.

This book focuses primarily on the informational aspects of management control systems—the levers managers use to transmit and process information within organizations. For the discussion to follow, I adopt the following definition of management control systems: *management control systems are the formal, information-based routines and procedures managers use to maintain or alter patterns in organizational activities.*

Several features of this definition are important. First, I am concerned primarily with *formal* routines and procedures—such as plans, budgets, and market share monitoring systems—although we will also examine how these stimulate informal processes that affect behavior. Second, management control systems are *information-based* systems. Senior managers use information for various purposes: to signal the domain in which subordinates should search for opportunities, to communicate plans and goals, to monitor the achievement of plans and goals, and to keep informed and inform others of emerging developments (Figure 1.1).

These information-based systems become control systems when they are used to maintain or alter *patterns* in organizational activities. Desirable patterns include not only goal-oriented activities—ensuring that new stores open on schedule—but also patterns of unanticipated innovation—discovering that branch employees' experiments with the layout of a store have doubled expected sales figures. Employees can surprise, and management control systems must accommodate intended strategies as well as strategies that emerge from local experimentation and independent employee initiatives. Finally, I am concerned with the control systems used by managers, not the host of

Figure 1.1   Information Needs of Top Managers in Implementing Strategy

control systems used lower in the organization to coordinate and regulate operating activities (e.g., quality control procedures for repetitive operations).

Figure 1.2 introduces the framework for the book. Business strategy—how a firm competes and positions itself vis-à-vis its competitors—is at the core of the analysis. The second level introduces four key constructs that must be analyzed and understood for the successful implementation of strategy: core values, risks to be avoided, critical performance variables, and strategic uncertainties. Each construct is controlled by a different system, or lever, the use of which has different implications. These levers are:

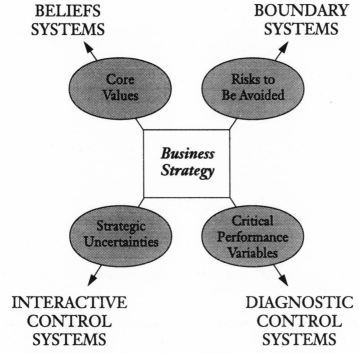

Figure 1.2 Controlling Business Strategy: Key Variables to Be Analyzed

1. beliefs systems, used to inspire and direct the search for new opportunities;
2. boundary systems, used to set limits on opportunity-seeking behavior;
3. diagnostic control systems, used to motivate, monitor, and reward achievement of specified goals; and
4. interactive control systems, used to stimulate organizational learning and the emergence of new ideas and strategies.

These four levers create the opposing forces—the yin and yang—of effective strategy implementation. In Chinese philosophy, positive and negative forces are opposing principles into which creative energy divides and whose fusion creates the world as we know it. Two of these control levers—beliefs systems and interactive control systems—create positive and inspirational forces. These are the yang: forces representing sun, warmth, and light. The other two levers—

boundary systems and diagnostic control systems—create constraints and ensure compliance with orders. These are the yin: forces representing darkness and cold. As I shall demonstrate, senior managers use these countervailing forces to achieve a dynamic tension that allows the effective control of strategy.

Selecting these levers—and using them properly—is a crucial decision for managers. Their choices reflect their personal values, reveal their opinions of subordinates, affect the probability of goal achievement, and influence the organization's long-term ability to adapt and prosper.

Controlling Business Strategy

Before we develop principles for controlling strategy, we must have a clear understanding of what we mean by the term *strategy*. Like the concept of control, the definition of strategy seems straightforward until we attempt to describe it in practice; then we find ourselves unconsciously slipping into and out of several different meanings. Henry Mintzberg (1987a) identifies at least four distinct ways the term may be used—as a plan, as a pattern of actions, as a competitive position, and as an overall perspective. As we shall see, each of these is controlled by a different lever.

The most familiar usage recognizes strategy as a plan, or a consciously intended course of action. This view ties in most strongly with the military's notion of strategy and tactics in which generals develop battle plans and issue instructions and field troops carry out orders. In this book, we examine the diagnostic control systems managers use to command and control through monitoring critical performance variables—the small number of variables essential to achieving intended business goals.

Strategy can be inferred from consistency in behavior, even if that consistency is not articulated in advance or even intended. Henry Ford offered his Model T only in black in the United States (and blue in Canada). Was this observable consistency a strategy? As Mintzberg states,

Every time a journalist imputes a strategy to a corporation or to a government, and every time a manager does the same thing to a competitor or even to the senior management of his own firm, they are implicitly defining strategy as pattern in action—that is, inferring consistency in behavior and labeling it strategy. They may, of course, go further and impute intention to that consistency—that is, assume there is a plan behind the pattern. But that is an assumption, which may prove false.

Thus, the definitions of strategy as plan and pattern can be quite independent of each other: plans may go unrealized, while patterns may appear without preconception. To paraphrase Hume, strategies may result from human actions but not human designs. (1987a, 13)

Managers control emerging patterns of action, often created by spontaneous employee initiatives, by using interactive control systems to focus attention on strategic uncertainties—uncertainties that could undermine the current basis of competitive advantage.

The view of strategy as position recognizes that firms choose different ways to compete in a product market. They may focus on differentiation of products, low cost, or specific customer groups (Porter 1980). Strategy as position focuses on the content, or economic substance, of the chosen strategy. Automobile manufacturers, for example, may choose to win market share by competing on either design features (BMW) or price (Hyundai). Managers attempt to control strategic position by using boundary systems to focus organizational attention on risks to be avoided—the identifiable, potentially severe risks that accompany choices about how to compete in chosen product markets.

Finally, many organizations such as Nike, Hewlett-Packard, and McDonald's view the world in a way that is embedded in their history and culture. For these organizations, strategy can be analyzed as a unique perspective or way of doing things. Strategy in this respect is to the organization as personality is to the individual.

This [final] definition suggests above all that strategy is a *concept*. This has one important implication, namely, that all strategies are abstractions which exist only in the minds of interested parties. It is important to remember that no one has ever seen a strategy or touched one; every strategy is an invention, a figment of someone's imagination, whether conceived of as intentions to regulate behavior before it takes place or inferred patterns to describe behavior that has already occurred.

What is of key importance about this [final] definition, however, is that the perspective is *shared*. As implied in the words Weltanschauung (German for "worldview"), culture, and ideology . . . strategy is a perspective shared by the members of an organization, through their intentions and/or by their actions. In effect, when we are talking of strategy in this context, we are entering the realm of the *collective mind*—individuals united by common thinking and/or behavior. A major issue of strategy formation becomes, therefore, how to read that collective mind—to understand how intentions diffuse through the system called organization to become shared and how actions come to be exercised on a collective yet consistent basis. (Mintzberg 1987a, 16–17)

To control this aspect of strategy, managers employ beliefs systems to communicate and control core values—the shared purpose of the business.

Implementing strategy effectively requires a balance among the four levers of control. This balance permits the simultaneous management of strategy as plan, pattern, position, and perspective. While management scholars have paid a great deal of attention to strategy formation, the control of strategy—that is, the control of the *processes* of strategy formation and implementation—has been relatively neglected. This book, then, presents an integrated theory for the control of strategy and illustrates the levers that turn theory to practice.

Organization of the Book

Managing the ongoing operations of any business and, at the same time, allowing sufficient innovation to adapt to changing markets is one of the basic challenges of management. In the chapters that follow, we shall examine how managers achieve a balance between the two by using the four basic levers of control. Chapter 2 lays the groundwork by analyzing the design fundamentals and key assumptions of strategy, organizations, and control. Tensions resulting from opportunity-seeking, limited attention, self-interest, and strategy formation are the focus of this chapter.

Part II, comprising chapters 3, 4, and 5, introduces and develops the basic levers of control. These chapters articulate the strategy constructs that must be controlled and the various types of control systems senior managers use. Chapter 3 examines the countervailing forces generated by beliefs systems and boundary systems. Chapter 4 discusses diagnostic control systems, performance measurement, and goal achievement. Chapter 5 illustrates how interactive control systems can be used to stimulate learning about strategic uncertainties.

Part III, encompassing chapters 6 and 7, analyzes the dynamics of controlling business strategy. Chapter 6 reports an empirical study of ten newly appointed chief executive officers and their use of control systems as levers of strategic renewal. Chapter 7 knits the arguments together by illustrating the dynamic tensions that are the key to understanding how senior managers use these techniques to control business strategy. Finally, two appendixes conclude the analysis: Appendix A offers a summary checklist of the "what," "why," "how," "when," and "who" of the four basic control levers; Appendix B discusses the use and misuse of information technology in applying these concepts in practice.

Any theory of management control must be evaluated on three dimensions:

1. the extent to which potentially important variables are included in the theory,
2. the clarity of the linkage between control system variables and the achievement of organizational strategies, and
3. the reliability and validity of the evidence. (Merchant and Simons 1986)

The framework presented here is derived from theory and ongoing research. Evidence is provided whenever possible by reference to empirical research and examples of practice. Good theory is falsifiable,[1] so testable propositions are offered throughout the book.

Everyone familiar with organizations knows implicitly that myriad control systems influence day-to-day operations. But there is little systematic understanding of why or how managers use these systems to accomplish their agendas. A useful typology codifies previously independent phenomena and allows prediction of relationships that are not connected in obvious ways (Tiryakian 1968, 178). My purpose in developing this framework, therefore, is to derive a set of propositions and predictive statements useful to both researchers and managers.

By the end of the book, readers will have a clear understanding of how and why effective managers use control systems for strategy implementation. For researchers the analysis lays out an integrated theory and testable hypotheses. For managers the theory and examples provide insight about practical techniques for controlling business strategy.

---

[1]One can never prove a hypothesis to be true since competing explanations can always exist. One can, however, demonstrate a theory or hypothesis to be false by observing circumstances in which predictions from the theory do not hold.

CHAPTER 2

A Balancing Act:
Tensions to Be Managed

This chapter introduces the tensions that arise in attempting to align organizations, business strategy, and human behavior. Balancing these tensions is at the heart of implementing strategy.

In a pure sense, organizations are instruments created to achieve specific goals such as the manufacture of machinery or the provision of services. But organizations are multifaceted. They are also social systems, collections of individuals bound together to meet personal and social needs. Group norms and patterns of power and influence affect internal decision processes. Organizations are also sets of relationships among self-interested participants, each of whom is balancing personal well-being and organizational needs.

Taken alone, each facet yields an incomplete picture of an organization. Viewing any organization as exclusively an instrument or a social system or a collection of self-interested individuals ignores important dimensions. An effective theory of control must admit multiple and simultaneous conceptions of organizational functioning.

Underlying the theory of this book are three organizational dynamics that reflect different facets of organizations: (1) the dynamics of creating value, (2) the dynamics of strategy making, and (3) the dynamics of human behavior. Each of these dynamics leads to organizational tensions that must be reconciled and balanced to allow the effective control of business strategy.

The Dynamics of Creating Value

As a starting point, let me propose that the *raison d'être* of any organization is to band together individuals who can identify opportunities and mobilize available resources to transform those opportunities into outputs of value. Organizations are created to serve a purpose. Typically they are created by individuals who believe that working with others to achieve a common goal is more desirable than working alone. Once created, however, the right of any organization to exist is not perpetual but must be earned.

An organization maintains its right to exist only as long as it can, with distinctive competence, turn a set of opportunities into goods or services valued by society. Distinctive competence implies that the organization is effective and efficient in both an absolute sense and in terms of competing organizations. Over time, the village hardware store may be displaced by the discount home improvement center; the major airline may be displaced by regional start-ups. Firms that cannot turn opportunities into value—as determined by the market—will be replaced by organizations that can.

Balancing Opportunity and Attention

Opportunity. Business scholars, notably economists, have long recognized that decision makers are constrained by the opportunities available to them. The study of economics is primarily the study of choice among a restricted set of opportunities (Arrow 1974, 17). In this analysis, however, we consider opportunity from a different perspective. For managers today, the problem is not one of constrained opportunity, it is one of too many opportunities. Stated simply, organizations face unlimited opportunity. Thus, the need to stimulate and control opportunities is a cornerstone of this analysis of business strategy and control.

Managers encounter opportunities from every direction: new projects are initiated by employees, a competitor proposes a joint venture, markets open in eastern Europe, government operations are privatized and bids are solicited, customers approach with special requests, a résumé from someone with special skills arrives in the mail, tariffs with Mexico fall, a technology breakthrough creates product design options not previously possible. Unexpected opportunities burst forth every day. Some are recognized, others are missed. Some are acted upon, others are passed over.

Research on innovation has helped us to understand the importance of creativity, experimentation, and surprise in organizational adaptation.[1] Individuals in organizations are not constrained to an exogenous opportunity set, as some might argue. Individuals can *create* opportunities. An unrelated thought or a story in the morning newspaper comes up in a discussion with a colleague or customer and leads to a new market initiative; something that has worked somewhere else is tried in a new area; discussions bring focus to new ideas; a customer request leads to prototypes and tests. Small ideas can become unexpected successes.

Since the creation of modern business organizations at the turn of the century, individuals in both small and large organizations have demonstrated incredible abilities to innovate, create opportunities, and define solutions to problems.[2] Daft and Becker, in their study of administrative innovation concluded,

The stream of innovation ideas into and through the organization exists independent of problems. Ideas may be brought into the organization by new personnel, or they may be discovered by existing personnel. Innovation solutions may occasionally be invented within the organization. Organization members may be attracted to certain ideas and push these ideas for adoption. Attraction to an idea may cause the member to look for a problem to which the innovation can be attached as a solution, or the participant may present the ideas as an opportunity for improved organizational performance. Under conditions of uncertainty ideas can be tried in order to learn whether they are preferable to existing procedures. (1978, 168–69)

Decisions are made when a problem or opportunity happens to collide with a set of people and a set of feasible solutions. James March and his colleagues have likened organizational decision making to a process in which problems, opportunities, solutions, and resources are mixed together in a "garbage can" (Cohen, March, and Olsen 1972; March and Weissinger-Baylon 1986). Outcomes may be surprising and may seem random or unpredictable. At one point in time, with a given set of people and a given frame of reference, one decision may emerge; at a different point in time with a different set of people, the "garbage can" may provide a different decision.

To aid in the analysis of later chapters, I introduce now the

---

[1] See, for example, Burns and Stalker (1961); Hedberg, Nystrom, and Starbuck (1976); and the collection of papers edited by March 1988, especially chs. 9 and 12.

[2] The propensity and efficiency of innovation in large versus small organizations and the point of diminishing returns to research and development spending are topics that have been actively debated and researched. See, for example, Ettlie, Bridges, and O'Keefe (1984) and the essays contained in Rosenbloom (1985).

construct of *opportunity space*, which I define as the unique set of opportunities that an organization can potentially identify or create at a point in time given its competencies and resources. This definition recognizes that individuals can augment an exogenously determined set of opportunities by creating opportunities. The opportunity space for an organization at any given point in time is determined by a variety of factors: innovation potential within the firm, existing asset and customer base, organizational skills and competencies, and anticipated reactions to market moves by competitors, suppliers, and customers. Industry history and structure also help to determine the opportunities available to a firm (Porter 1980). For example, firms operating in fragmented industries, such as home heating oil delivery firms, have different opportunities than firms in highly concentrated industries, such as electric utilities.

Moreover, the historical evolution of firms within industries influences competencies, resources, and opportunities. After the maturation of an industry, first movers with established product markets face choices that are different from the choices of late entrants with new products or technologies. Large-scale capital asset decisions made years earlier often constrain a firm to certain sets of opportunities (Ghemawat 1991). Due to past choices and positioning, competitors such as Wal-Mart and Sears operate in different opportunity spaces, and, as a result, their tactical options are dramatically different. Major photography film companies such as Eastman Kodak similarly find themselves in a unique position determined by history. They have built world-scale chemical processing plants in the past and therefore are committed to chemical-based processes at a time when digital-imaging technology is poised to reshape the industry.

Limited attention. While it is difficult to specify the conditions under which the identification or creation of opportunities will occur, we can state that innovations and solutions cannot be created without organizational attention. Therefore, organizational attention is critical to creating value. From an individual perspective, attention is the set of elements that enters consciousness at any point in time (Simon 1976, 90); organizational attention refers to the allocation of information processing capacity within the organization to a defined issue or agenda.

Decisions are an outcome of stimuli that channel attention to specific sets of issues (Simon 1976, 91). The transformation of available resources into outputs of value requires the attention of individuals. A new idea cannot be brought to market unless individuals devote time and attention to it. But attention is a scarce resource that must be rationed across opportunities. Individuals are not computers. We have limited cognitive information processing capacity. Organizational participants must use information processing tricks—heuristics, standard operating procedures, and rules-of-thumb—to filter away excess complexity and extraneous signals (Cyert and March 1963, 102–113). As Herbert Simon notes,

The information-processing systems of our contemporary world swim in an exceedingly rich soup of information, of symbols. In a world of this kind, the scarce resource is not information; it is processing capacity to attend to information. Attention is the chief bottleneck in organizational activity, and the bottleneck becomes narrower and narrower as we move to the top of organizations. (1976, 294)

Organizations cannot attend to all goals simultaneously (Cyert and March 1963, 35); therefore, organizational attention is a fundamental constraint in achieving objectives. Managers have many demands on their time. They must allocate their attention across multiple roles as figureheads, leaders, liaisons, monitors, information disseminators, spokesmen, entrepreneurs, disturbance handlers, resource allocators, and negotiators (Mintzberg 1973, 167–69). Given the limited attention of organizational participants and the unlimited opportunities facing organizations, it is imperative to focus organizational attention in productive ways. My colleague John Kotter argues, in fact, that focusing organizational attention on agendas linked to explicit business strategies is one of the primary hallmarks of effective general managers (1982, 60–66).

Maximizing return-on-management. A fundamental problem in creating value, therefore, is balancing unlimited opportunity with limited attention. To transform opportunity space into outputs of value, managers must find ways to leverage the limited attention of their organizations. Opportunity-seeking must be directed and focused. Employees must be given cues about what to pay attention to; they must be encouraged to create the right kind of opportunities.

Given scarce management attention and unlimited opportunity, managers need to know how to maximize return-on-management, or "ROM." We are skilled in analyzing ROI, return-on-investment, to determine how to maximize cash flows for given levels of assets employed, but the most critical constraint is not financial, nor informational, nor technological. The most critical constraint is management attention. If enough smart people focus their attention on a set of issues, almost any obstacle can be overcome, almost any opportunity

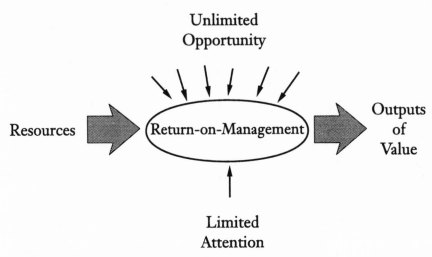

Figure 2.1   Balancing Opportunity and Attention

can be turned to advantage, but to maximize ROM, attention must be conserved for the most critical opportunities. The routine operations of the organization must be able to occur without constant management oversight.

In the analysis to follow, we will consider how management control systems can reconcile the inherent tension between attention and opportunity, thereby allowing managers to maximize ROM to create value (Figure 2.1).

The Dynamics of Strategy Making

Most current definitions of control refer to the strategy process in the same way. Roberty Anthony, for example, defines management control as "the process by which managers influence other members of the organization to implement the organization's strategies" (1988, 10).[3] Lorange, Scott Morton, and Goshal define a strategic control system as "a system to support managers in assessing the relevance of the organization's strategy to its progress in the accom-

[3] In his influential original monograph *Planning and Control Systems: A Framework for Analysis*, published in 1965, Anthony defined management control as "the process by which managers assure that resources are obtained and used effectively and efficiently in the accomplishment of the organization's objectives" (p. 17). This shift in definition represents, at least to some extent, the increased importance accorded to the concept of strategy in the intervening decades.

plishment of its goals and, where discrepancies exist, to support areas needing attention (1986, 10).

Two critical assumptions are implicit in these definitions. First, management control systems are tools for implementing business strategies. Second, strategy formation is a top-down process. Figure 2.2 illustrates this hierarchical conception of strategy and the management control process.

In the hierarchical model, which could also be labeled the military model of command and control, senior managers formulate strategies and communicate these strategies down the organization hierarchy. These strategies, which are called intended strategies, are recorded and communicated in formal planning documents. Middle managers and the operating core of the organization implement the strategies. Management control systems then measure progress, which is monitored by senior managers who may need to take corrective action.

There are several implicit assumptions in a hierarchical view of the strategy process: strategies are deliberate and intentional; strategies are articulated in advance of implementation; formulation is separate from implementation; strategy making is reserved for top management; and strategy equals a plan (Mintzberg 1987a, 1987b, 1990).

In this view, strategy formation is analytical and conceptual. To formulate the correct strategy, a manager must have good data and sound reasoning. Over the last decade, therefore, management theorists have devoted more attention to techniques for developing good strategies than to techniques for implementing them. For these theorists, breaking strategy into action plans seems fairly straightforward.

A study of the strategy process in actual organizations, however, casts doubt on some of the assumptions in the hierarchical view. Research in firms as disparate as airlines, automobile manufacturers,

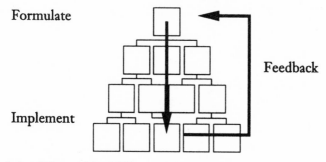

Figure 2.2   Hierarchical View of Strategy

film studios, and supermarket chains reveals that strategies often flow from the bottom of the organization upward.[4] Honda successfully invaded the United States motorcycle market not by careful planning in Japan, but rather because Japanese managers in the United States sensed unanticipated demand for 50cc motorcycles. The intended strategy was to sell the large motorcycles that U.S. customers seemed to prefer. But when the 250cc and 305cc motorcycles failed to attract customer interest because of quality problems, local managers capitalized on the consumer interest aroused by the 50cc motorcycles they drove to work. As sales of smaller motorcycles increased, a sustainable strategy emerged (Pascale 1984).

In a similar way, a simple change in packaging led to a new strategy in a business that sold accessories to shoe stores. Shoe trees had been sold exclusively in retail shoe stores to complement a shoe sale transaction. To better display the product, a new window package was introduced. This created an unanticipated opportunity for the marketing salesforce to experiment by placing the product in other retail outlets. Before long, high-volume mass merchandisers became the cornerstone of a redefined strategy. In turn, new products were developed for this market and successfully introduced.[5]

Neither of these strategies was intended. Instead, each strategy was the result of local attempts to capitalize on emerging opportunities that were not anticipated when plans were formalized. When successful and replicated, these spontaneous actions coalesced into viable business strategies.

In this emergent, or incremental, view, strategy can emerge from all levels of the organization as individuals search for and create opportunities (Figure 2.3). Several assumptions underlie the emergent view of the strategy process: strategies are incremental and emerge over time; intended strategies are often superseded; formulation and implementation are often intertwined; strategic decisions occur throughout the organization; and strategy equals a process

Balancing Intended Strategy and
Emergent Strategy

Although the hierarchical model and emergent model offer competing views of the strategy process, they are not mutually exclusive. In

---

[4]See Bower (1970, ch. 9); Mintzberg (1978); Quinn (1980); Mintzberg and Waters (1982); Pascale (1984).

[5]From a paper prepared by Bill Fry and Jeff Hendren for the Harvard M.B.A. course Strategic Management Systems, 1990.

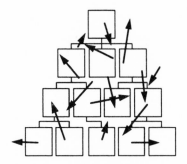

Figure 2.3   Emergent View of Strategy

observing how managers craft strategy, Henry Mintzberg suggests that both models operate simultaneously in organizations:

In practice, of course, all strategy making walks on two feet, one deliberate, the other emergent. For just as purely deliberate strategy making precludes learning, so purely emergent strategy making precludes control. Pushed to the limit, neither approach makes much sense.

Likewise, there is no such thing as a purely deliberate strategy or a purely emergent one. No one organization—not even the ones commanded by those ancient Greek generals—knows enough to work everything out in advance, to ignore learning en route. And no one—not even a solitary potter—can be flexible enough to leave everything to happenstance, to give up all control (1987b, 69).

Under these circumstances, a theory for controlling strategy must accommodate both hierarchical and emergent models. One minute, an executive is meeting to determine if sales and market share goals are being achieved; the next minute, he receives a telephone call informing him that an unauthorized change in product specifications has created a surge in demand from new customers. Organizational participants work diligently to implement desired plans at the same time they are turning unexpected opportunities to advantage. As we shall see, balancing control and learning is critical to managing the tension between efficiency and innovation.

The Dynamics of Human Motives

Every theory of management makes assumptions about human behavior. The accepted view of human behavior in organizations has changed dramatically over this century. Frederick Taylor's work *Principles of Scientific Management*, published in 1911, likened individual workers to machines that could be fine-tuned in pursuit of efficiency. Using time-and-motion studies, Taylor raised the acts of shovelling and handling pig-iron to a science. Managers were enjoined to study repetitive tasks carefully or hire experts to do so, to experiment to improve prescribed procedures continually, and to ensure that workers complied with these practices by offering piece rate incentives. In Taylor's view, workers would only respond to financial incentives based on defined performance standards.

Twenty years later, Elton Mayo's research at the Hawthorne Works of the Western Electric Company caused him to rebel against what he called the "rabble hypothesis" that underlay economic incentives and controls. According to Mayo, there were three assumptions girding the economic theory that were demonstrably false: "(1) natural society consists of a horde of unorganized individuals; (2) every individual acts in a manner calculated to secure his self-interest; (3) every individual thinks logically, to the best of his ability, in the service of this aim" (1949, 37). Mayo asserted, "In their behavior and their statements, economists indicate that they accept the rabble hypothesis and its dismal corollary of financial incentive as the only effective human motive. They substitute a logical hypothesis of small practical value for the actual facts" (p. 74).

Mayo's research lay the ground work for an emphasis on human relationships in organizations. As a result of his studies, Mayo argued that worker performance was linked to social interaction in the work place. Emotions, group norms, and sentiment flowing from association with groups were critical variables in motivating and guiding human behavior. Managers were advised to maximize human potential by providing supportive environments. Mayo and his proponents argued that job satisfaction would lead to increased performance more readily than any attempt to standardize tasks and offer rate incentives. In the 1960s, other academic authors, notably Douglas McGregor and Rensis Likert, built on this theme to differentiate authoritative, nonparticipatory management styles from more participative, caring styles, which they argued were superior in unleashing human initiative.

In the 1950s and 1960s, Abraham Maslow and Frederick Herzberg attempted to reconcile the performance implications of economic incentives with the social aspects of work place behavior. These authors distinguished between physical/security needs and emotional/psychological needs. Maslow posited a hierarchy of needs, ranging from basic safety and security to self-esteem and self-actualization.

Under Maslow's theory, a need ceased to be a motivator once it was satisfied; thus, material incentives were no longer motivators for most workers who had stable, well-paying jobs. Instead, improved performance was a function of increased opportunities for self-esteem and self-actualization. In a similar vein, Herzberg carried out a series of studies suggesting that the causes of job satisfaction were independent of the causes of job dissatisfaction. According to Herzberg, safety and security needs, for example, could cause job dissatisfaction if inadequate but did not, in themselves, create job satisfaction if provided in ample amounts. Instead, job satisfaction derived from situations in which workers could feel a sense of accomplishment and personal growth. Underlying the work of both Maslow and Herzberg was the assumption that increased job satisfaction leads to increased performance.

Human motives in organizations were deemphasized in the 1960s and 1970s, as management theorists became interested in the decision-making capacity of organizations as collective units. Individuals were assumed to bargain with each other to produce acceptable organizational goals, "satisfice" in their attempt to maximize personal utility, and use heuristics to solve problems (Cyert and March 1963). Under this "behavioral theory of the firm," the organization—rather than the individual—is the primary unit of analysis, and it is assumed that people act to achieve the goals of the organization.

In the mid-1970s and 1980s, economists became interested in the internal workings of organizations. Viewing organizations as internal markets, economists constructed theories based on performance contracts and the exchange of property rights between self-interested agents (employees) and their superiors (principals). These theories reintroduced the "rabble" assumptions of individual action.

Using mathematical formulations of utility functions, economists assume that individuals are rational, self-interested, calculating, utility-maximizing agents who experience disutility in work-related efforts (Jensen and Meckling 1976; Holmström, 1979; Fama and Jensen 1983; Jensen 1983). Economists see opportunity-seeking in a special way:

Opportunistic behavior is any action engaged in by an exchange partner, enjoying an informational (or some other) advantage to exploit that advantage to the economic detriment of others. In its crassest form, opportunism is "lying, stealing, and cheating" (Williamson, 1975). In its more subtle forms, opportunism can be raising the price of your good or service once your customer has irreversibly committed to buy from you, lowering your quality in the same circumstances, or demanding other concessions when you enjoy some economic advantage (Barney and Ouchi 1986, 19).

In the economic theory of organizations, without monitoring and negative sanctions, self-interested individuals will avoid effort and shirk required duties. Research supporting this view relies heavily on large sample statistics linking corporate behavior to the structure of bonus incentives to impute central tendencies of individual action in organizations.[6]

Reconciling Self-Interest with the Desire to Contribute

Reconciling these divergent assumptions about human behavior is a fundamental problem in developing or applying theories of management. It requires recognition of what I call the paradox of central tendency: we cannot manage effectively unless we understand central tendencies, yet central tendencies do not provide lessons on managing. To illustrate, consider an example in which the empirical evidence shows that 70 percent of individuals in organizations shirk their duties in the absence of monitoring and incentives. How should we interpret this central tendency? Is it due to innate human nature? Is it due to individual traits? Or, is it due to a lack of leadership and direction? What of the 30 percent who do not shirk? Is shirking a result of unproductive organizational forces that reduce an individual's desire to contribute productively?

Economists would argue that the data supports the assumption that individuals are innately self-interested and find disutility in effort. The economic theory of organizations is a positive theory—that is, one that attempts to describe the world as it functions. Great care must be exercised, however, since positive theories can easily be reified to serve as blueprints for action. As Chris Argyris reminds us, "all descriptive concepts, once they are used to organize reality and guide behavior, become normative" (1973, 265). If theory slips from a description of central tendencies to a normative checklist for action, managers may be advised to write incentive contracts as if all employees were self-interested and exhibited disutility in effort. But brand-

---

[6]For examples of this type of empirical research, see special issues of the *Journal of Accounting and Economics* devoted to "Management Compensation and The Managerial Labor Market" 7, nos. 1–3 (1985) and "Accounting and the Theory of the Firm" 12, nos. 1–3 (1990).

ing individuals with the average traits of a group is always dangerous, especially in organizations where leadership and management action play key roles. As descriptive theories, central tendencies unquestionably yield important insights, but they should not become checklists for action.

Social psychologists often find themselves on the opposite side of this paradox. By studying effective and ineffective groups and social systems, these researchers concentrate on understanding the forces that allow individuals to perform to their potential or prevent them from doing so. Their theories focus on the emotions, aspirations, achievements, and social behavior of individuals and groups. As a result, their research does not usually rely on large data bases that permit statistics based on central tendencies. Thus, their work may fail to identify the deeper forces at work in business organizations and the equilibrium that will derive in the absence of managerial actions.

To unlock the paradox of central tendency, effective managers must understand central tendency and manage against it. Effective managers do not work to achieve average outcomes. In highly competitive markets, average behavior can never be a sustainable goal. Managers must move their organizations and the people who work in them away from the mean toward the upper tail of the distribution. The essence of business strategy is to do something distinctive: distinctive individuals; distinctive capabilities; distinctive market positions. To prosper in rapidly changing, highly competitive markets, managers must rely on the imagination and initiative of employees and must attract and develop talented individuals. Returning to our earlier example, the 30 percent who exhibited productive contribution should be the focus of our interest.

An exclusive focus on central tendencies attaches too much importance to the undifferentiated average actions of the group, but at the same time, we cannot ignore central tendencies. Attention is limited, and without intervention, central tendencies will prevail. In the absence of management action, self-interested behavior at the expense of organizational goals is inevitable. Argyris's (1985) work on defensive routines is one of the few attempts to reconcile the paradox of central tendency. Argyris's research recognizes that organizations have central tendencies but notes that many of these are caused by nonproductive forces. At the core of Argyris's work is an attempt to identify these nonproductive forces so that managers can eliminate them and thereby increase the human potential to contribute.

To reconcile the conflicting views about human behavior in organizations, I will use a two-stage process to articulate the assumptions that underlie my theory of control. First-stage assumptions concern the basic human traits that can be observed in organizational settings. These assumptions are driven by the view that individuals in organizations are opportunity-seekers. Most theories of organization assume that people react to situations or choices that are presented to them. The analysis that follows pays special attention to the potential of innate curiosity and independent initiative that distinguishes the human spirit. Triggered by cues and stimuli in the environment, human beings are intrinsically motivated to create situations of advantage by seeking and/or creating opportunity. In the absence of allegiances or commitment to others, opportunity-seeking behavior may be purely self-interested behavior, but strong leaders and worthwhile causes create forces that influence the direction of opportunity-seeking.

Counteracting these forces are second-stage assumptions about organizational blocks that can derail productive opportunity-seeking. Stultifying rules, sanctions for errors, group pressures, and the fear of embarrassment or failure are all blocks to opportunity-seeking. Managers use control systems to enforce positive human traits and overcome organizational blocks, thereby reducing the pull toward central tendencies and capturing the benefits of organizational search and innovation.

Let us consider these first-stage assumptions and their related organizational blocks.

1. The desire to do right. I assume that individuals in organizations have a code of personal conduct that makes them want to act in an ethical manner. Our society has highly developed mechanisms to transmit codes of personal conduct: family teaching, religious teaching, youth groups, and benevolent associations all work to internalize values related to ethical behaviors. As an individual grows and develops, these values are internalized (Kohlberg and Turiel 1973). Moreover, social sanctions and peer disapproval are constant reminders of the limits of acceptable behavior.

Organizational blocks. Business organizations often provide opportunities for individuals to make decisions that conflict with codes of personal conduct. First, as a collection of assets and a stream of cash flows, business organizations offer temptations to individuals who, for reasons of personal circumstance, may find excuses to divert assets to personal use. If individuals believe that no one is hurt by these actions, the temptations are magnified. Second, organizations bring a variety of pressures—to conform, to deliver expected results, to grant favors—to bear on individuals that may cause them to act against personal moral codes.

2. *The desire to achieve and contribute.* I assume that individuals in organizations seek achievement for two reasons. First, achievement brings tangible rewards—money, prestige, promotion. Second, individuals value personal achievement as a reward in itself. Even without tangible benefits, individuals value the satisfaction derived from personal accomplishment and contribution. Individuals experience positive utility from contributing to team efforts. Much of the modern research in psychology and social psychology confirms this assumption. Why would 50 percent of American adults work as volunteers in nonprofit organizations, giving up on average five hours per week, if not for the satisfaction of contributing to something they perceive as worthwhile (Drucker 1989)?

Organizational blocks. Business organizations often reduce opportunities for personal achievement and contribution. First, individuals may be unsure of how to make a contribution that will be recognized, valued, and rewarded. They may not be sure of what the organization wants them to do. Second, individuals may feel the pressures of competing tasks. Achievement requires focused effort, but focusing on too many things dilutes an individual's impact and reduces the potential for achievement. As performance demands increase, attention remains finite. Finally, the organization may fail to provide sufficient resources to allow achievement.

3. *The desire to create.* The opportunity space of a business organization permits a great deal of creativity and choice of action. I assume that individuals have innate potential to innovate, experiment, and create. If given the chance, many employees will fulfil this potential. Innate curiosity and desire to find a better way are powerful human forces, and innovation and experimentation create the novelty and interest that make work enjoyable. Opportunities coupled with creativity become new products, processes, and relationships.[7]

Organizational blocks. Business organizations sometimes stifle the desire of individuals to create. First, due to task constraints or re-

---

[7] For research relating to innovation in organizations, see the Research Annual Series, *Research on Technological Innovation, Management and Policy*, edited by R.S. Rosenbloom. For an analysis of organizational factors affecting innovation, see Amabile and Gryskiewicz (1988). For a senior manager's perspective, see Taylor (1990).

source limitations, individuals may lack the opportunity to exercise their creative energies. Identified opportunities may not be acted upon because it is thought the resources needed will be difficult to obtain. Second, individuals may fear risks in challenging the accepted ways of doing things. Challenging the status quo may threaten vested interests and bring censure or retaliation. New ideas may conflict with existing wisdom or, worse, with the statements or views of superiors. New ideas may reveal errors in past and current actions. Agreeing with group opinions or opinion leaders is safer than challenging conventional thinking. Third, opportunity-seeking behavior in business organizations may lack guidance. Individuals who are unsure of the type of opportunities to seize will tend to miss important opportunities. At the same time, these individuals may pursue a variety of unfocused initiatives that collectively risk dissipating the resources of the organization.

The model of human behavior that emerges from these assumptions is multifaceted. All of us who work inside organizations value achievement and tangible rewards as well as the ability to contribute and to be creative in our work. We are predisposed to follow actions in harmony with the moral codes of our society, but organizations create many obstacles that can derail or impede these productive forces.

The Dynamics of Controlling Business Strategy

Effective managers use control systems selectively to balance the inherent tensions between (1) unlimited opportunity and limited attention, (2) intended and emergent strategy, and (3) self-interest and the desire to contribute. Underlying these tensions is the desire to do right, to achieve, to contribute, and to create. To unleash this potential, managers must overcome organizational blocks. Management control systems play an important role in this process:

- To reduce the risk of temptation or pressure, management control systems are used selectively to specify and enforce the organization's rules of the game.
- To bring focus and resources to individuals seeking the opportu-

nity to achieve, management control systems are used selectively to build and support clear stretch targets.

- To stimulate innovation, management control systems are used selectively to inspire and motivate organizational participants to create and search for new opportunities.
- To reduce the fear of challenging the status quo, management control systems are used selectively to open organizational debate and dialogue and thereby trigger organizational learning.

Control of business strategy, then, is more than ensuring the implementation of plans. Control implies managing the inherent tension between creative innovation, on the one hand, and predictable goal achievement, on the other, so that both are transformed into profitable growth. Effective control of strategy requires both the freedom to innovate and the assurance that individuals are working productively toward predefined goals.

Beliefs systems, boundary systems, diagnostic control systems, and interactive control systems are the four basic levers used to manage this tension. The four levers are nested, and each offers some measure of guidance to the strategy process. Beliefs systems and interactive systems expand and define the opportunity space of the firm. Boundary systems and diagnostic systems constrain and focus attention on strategic domains and opportunities.

Since management attention is limited, staff experts play an important role in balancing the attention or inattention of managers. In later chapters, we will examine how the role of staff experts varies according to the nature and purpose of the different levers.

Summary

In this chapter, I have stated key assumptions about organizations, strategy, and human motivations. Three major themes will recur. First, control systems are important levers in managing the inherent tension between opportunity-seeking behavior and limited attention. Balancing this tension is essential to maximizing return-on-management and creating outputs of value. Second, there is an interaction between intended strategy processes and emergent strategy processes. Both are important. Third, management control systems are capable of reconciling tensions between individual self-interest and innate desires to contribute. We must understand how managers use the four control levers selectively to overcome organizational blocks and unlock the potential for opportunity-seeking. As I shall demonstrate in Part III, the selective use of these levers relies on the continual interplay between positive and negative forces—motivation and coercion, reward and punishment, guidance and proscription, learning and control—to create a dynamic tension between goal achievement and creative innovation.

PART II

Basic Levers of Control

Beliefs and Boundaries:
Framing the Strategic Domain

How do managers control the search for opportunities? There are two control levers that guide search activity in organizations: beliefs systems and boundary systems. Both are variations on formal control systems. One is a positive system that motivates the search for opportunities; the other is a negative system that constrains the search. Neither system is cybernetic; that is, neither system relies on the routine feedback of variance information to correct a process. Nevertheless, by providing momentum and a domain for organizational search activity, beliefs systems and boundary systems form the foundation for the more traditional cybernetic management control systems discussed in later chapters.

Beliefs Systems

Every organization is created for a purpose. In most organizations, that purpose is rooted in the articles of incorporation. Harvard University, for example, was founded in 1636 "to advance *Learning* and perpetuate it to Posterity; dreading to leave an illiterate Ministry to the Churches, when our present Ministers shall lie in the Dust."[1]

[1] This text was the first formal statement of purpose by the founding fathers of what was to become Harvard College. The passage, credited to President Dunster, is the opening paragraph of section two "In Respect of the Colledge, and the proceeding of *Learning* therein," from *New England's First Fruits*, published in 1643 and quoted in Morison (1935, 247, 304).

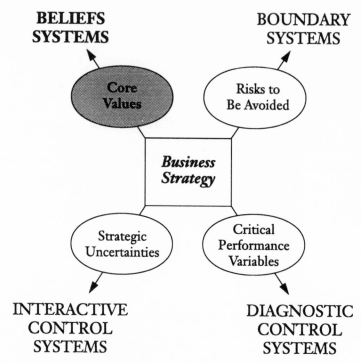

Figure 3.1   The First Lever of Control

During the formative stages of most organizations, frequent interaction among participants keeps the organization's purpose clear. As organizations grow and mature, however, defining and communicating a unified purpose becomes both more important and more difficult.

A beliefs system is the explicit set of organizational definitions that senior managers communicate formally and reinforce systematically to provide basic values, purpose, and direction for the organization. The definitions espouse the values and direction that senior managers want subordinates to adopt. These core values are linked to the business strategy of the firm (Figure 3.1).

A formal beliefs system is created and communicated through such documents as credos, mission statements, and statements of purpose. As an example, Exhibit 3.1 reproduces the Johnson & Johnson Credo. Beliefs systems attempt to convey information about core values: how the organization creates value ("Best Customer Service in the World"), the level of performance desired ("Pursuit of Excel-

Our Credo

We believe our first responsibility is to the doctors, nurses and patients,
to mothers and fathers and all others who use our products and services.
In meeting their needs everything we do must be of high quality.
We must constantly strive to reduce our costs
in order to maintain reasonable prices.
Customers' orders must be serviced promptly and accurately.
Our suppliers and distributors must have an opportunity
to make a fair profit.

We are responsible to our employees,
the men and women who work with us throughout the world.
Everyone must be considered as an individual.
We must respect their dignity and recognize their merit.
They must have a sense of security in their jobs.
Compensation must be fair and adequate,
and working conditions clean, orderly and safe.
We must be mindful of ways to help our employees fulfill
their family responsibilities.
Employees must feel free to make suggestions and complaints.
There must be equal opportunity for employment, development
and advancement for those qualified.
We must provide competent management,
and their actions must be just and ethical.

We are responsible to the communities in which we live and work
and to the world community as well.
We must be good citizens—support good works and charities
and bear our fair share of taxes.
We must encourage civic improvements and better health and education.
We must maintain in good order
the property we are privileged to use,
protecting the environment and natural resources.

Our final responsibility is to our stockholders.
Business must make a sound profit.
We must experiment with new ideas.
Research must be carried on, innovative programs developed
and mistakes paid for.
New equipment must be purchased, new facilities provided
and new products launched.
Reserves must be created to provide for adverse times.
When we operate according to these principles,
the stockholders should realize a fair return.

Johnson & Johnson

Exhibit 3.1   The Johnson & Johnson Credo

lence"), and how individuals are expected to manage relationships both internally and externally ("Respect for the Individual"). Mission statements, credos, and statements of purpose may be considered part of a system when they are (1) formal, (2) information-based, and (3) used by managers to maintain or alter patterns in organizational activities.

The primary purpose of a beliefs system is to inspire and guide organizational search and discovery. When problems arise in implementing strategy, a beliefs system helps participants to determine the types of problems to tackle and the solutions to search for. More important, in the absence of problems, beliefs systems motivate individuals to search for new ways of creating value.[2]

Organizational beliefs systems are created by the symbolic use of information. Great leaders and competent managers understand the power of symbolism and inspiration (Westley and Mintzberg 1989). As Feldman and March have noted, "at the individual level, symbols produce belief and belief stimulates the discovery of new realities" (1981, 180).

Formal beliefs systems are a recent organizational innovation. In a 1991 seminar, entitled "Achieving Breakthrough Service" held at Harvard Business School, sixty-eight out of seventy-two participants reported having formal mission statements or similar documents. When asked if their organizations had such documents fifteen years ago, only six answered yes. Several factors account for this trend. In the past, an organization's mission was tacit but well understood. There was little need to formalize organizational purpose because the products or services offered were designed to meet a specific demand in a defined market. Competitive strategies could be developed without reference to core values.

Today, businesses are more complex: firms combine multiple business units under the same corporate umbrella; global competition results in new strategic alliances; and rapidly changing information and production technologies now allow cross pollination of competitive processes, services, and products. In many companies and industries, this increasing complexity makes it difficult for individuals to comprehend organizational purpose and direction.

Furthermore, technology now bombards managers with data that

---

[2] The ability of a beliefs system to inspire creative search activity can be contrasted to problem-driven models of search behavior. Cyert and March, for example, develop a theory of problem-driven search (1963, 120–22). In their model, search behavior is activated to identify a solution to a perceived problem, defined as failure or anticipated failure to satisfy a goal.

force constant reassessment of their competitive positions. Managers must use this information to ensure that internal operations are efficient and effective. Downsizing and realignment are the new realities. This environment of constant challenge and change creates a need for strong basic values to provide organizational stability.

Finally, the modern work force has changed. Better educated participants with higher expectations desire personal challenge and the ability to contribute to a purposive endeavor. If managers are to transform individual abilities into cohesive organizational outputs, each individual must understand the organization's purpose and his or her contribution to that purpose. As managers look to empowered employees for new ideas and competitive advantages, this need to understand the organization's purpose grows in importance.

Although several authors have noted that middle managers are especially important in identifying and creating new strategic initiatives (Burgelman 1983a, b, c; Nonaka 1988), these managers will not become enthusiastic participants in the search for opportunity if they do not understand the beliefs of the organization and are not invited to participate in transforming those beliefs into actions and strategies (Westley 1990).

For managers who are engineering organizational change, formal beliefs systems are vital. "A new vision can help to attract and unite followers and galvanize them to high levels of effort. Because it is so different, a radical mission calls for new values and norms—new understandings about what is desirable and expected—as well as new belief and meaning systems." (Trice and Beyer 1991, 154–55). Still, many of the benefits of creating formal beliefs systems flow from the discussion necessary to communicate and understand these beliefs rather than from the credos and statements themselves. Through discussion, senior managers can increase the commitment of participants to organizational goals and mission.[3]

As the opportunity space of a business expands, the creation and communication of a formal beliefs system become more important. Managers attempt to define the values and direction of the organization by (1) asserting uniqueness, (2) providing prestige to group membership, and (3) using formal beliefs as symbols of what the organization represents. These actions are intended to increase commitment, provide a core of stability, and reinforce the distinctiveness of the organization (Ashforth and Mael 1989).

[3] For a senior manager's description of such a process, see Kanter (1991), p. 121.

John Kotter's study of leadership concluded that effective leaders are able to motivate and inspire organizational participants to bursts of energy in support of organizational goals and strategies. Using survey data and field interviews, Kotter concluded that inspirational motivation is created by (1) articulating a vision that addresses the values of participants, (2) allowing each individual to appreciate how he or she can contribute to the achievement of that vision, (3) providing enthusiastic support for effort, and (4) encouraging public recognition and reward for all successes (1990, 63). Beliefs systems play a central role in this process.

DiMaggio and Powell (1983) argue that managers faced with uncertainty may *mimic* successful organizations by adopting their systems and processes. Consultants, the popular business press, and industry associations supply models from other organizations for managers to copy. Thus, a new mission statement may result as direct mimicry of successful organizations that have mission statements. Moreover, some theorists have argued that the adoption of formal processes and structures such as beliefs systems may be an important legitimating action to demonstrate managerial competence (Meyer and Rowan 1977).

Human beings are intrinsically motivated to make commitments to others in personal relationships and in organizations. In these commitments, self-interest is often overridden or tempered by emotional needs (Frank 1988). Within organizations, commitment means believing in organizational values and being willing to exert effort to achieve broad organizational goals. In general, the higher the level of an individual's commitment, the higher the level of his or her performance.[4]

Beliefs systems, which are value-laden and inspirational, must be broad enough to allow all organizational participants to commit to organizational values and purpose on their own terms. A mission statement, for example, should appeal to a salesman, a manager, a production worker, and a clerical worker. Because they are broad and inspirational, however, beliefs systems cannot be tied to formal organizational incentives. They are too vague to use as standards against which performance can be measured. If a formal beliefs system is useful as a tool for providing inspiration and organizational direction, how do managers transform these vague beliefs into focused, purposive activity?

---

[4]For a review of literature on this topic, see Locke, Latham, and Erez (1988).

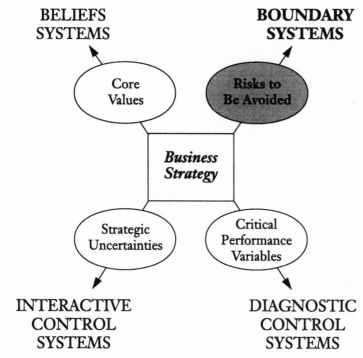

Figure 3.2   The Second Lever of Control

To answer this question, we must examine the role of another class of systems—boundary systems—that has not been documented previously. Boundary systems impose important limits on the organizational search activity motivated by beliefs systems.

Boundary Systems

Boundary systems, the second lever of control, delineate the acceptable domain of activity for organizational participants. Unlike beliefs systems, boundary systems do not specify positive ideals. Instead, they establish limits, based on defined business risks, to opportunity-seeking (Figure 3.2).

Individuals in organizations are opportunity-seekers; that is, when presented with new information and situations, they search for ways to create value or overcome obstacles. It is impossible for managers, in all but the simplest organizations to know all the problems, solutions, and opportunities organizational participants face.[5] Therefore, managers should not dictate the specific opportunities participants should seek.

Consider, for example, a small organization such as Harvard Business School. The 1,000 individuals employed by the school work to solve problems, create solutions, and identify new ways of performing their assigned tasks. Senior managers (the dean and associate deans) cannot possibly know all the potential problems, solutions, and opportunities that may be considered or constructed by each individual. Even if the problem of specific knowledge could be overcome, dictating how each individual should perform his or her tasks would destroy the personal initiative and experimentation that underlies creative search activity.

In critiquing classical decision theory, Christenson (1972) develops an essential, but overlooked, point: decision makers not only search for the highest value action from an array of actions, they also construct or invent acts that, prior to their invention, could not have been specified as decision alternatives. Nelson and Winter also recognize that search activity may result in the creation of alternatives not previously contemplated (1982, p. 171). Attempting to specify how individuals should perform their tasks *ex ante* precludes the invention of new opportunities that might create value.

On the one hand, then, the use of imprecise beliefs systems inspires unfocused search behaviors that risk dissipating the resources and energies of the firm. On the other hand, it is inappropriate for senior managers to specify in detail how participants should search for opportunity in the conduct of their work. Senior managers solve this dilemma by dictating what subordinates should *not* do and relying on individual creativity to search for ways of creating value within these boundaries.[6] Thus, boundary systems are usually stated in negative terms or as minimum standards.

Chester Barnard, writing more than fifty years ago, realized that setting limits on action was a prerequisite for effective organizational decision making. "The power of choice is paralyzed in human beings if the number of equal opportunities is large. . . . Limitation of possibilities is necessary to choice. Finding a reason why something should

---

[5] For a discussion of the limitations of centralized planning in complex decision systems, see Hayek (1978).

[6] My colleague Charles Christenson anticipates and develops this point for a somewhat different purpose in his paper "The Power of Negative Thinking" (1972).

not be done is a common method of deciding what should be done. The processes of decision as we shall see are largely techniques for narrowing choice" (1938, 14).

Although boundary systems are essentially proscriptive or negative systems, they allow managers to delegate decision making and thereby allow the organization to achieve maximum flexibility and creativity. In many ways, boundary systems are a prerequisite for organizational freedom and entrepreneurial behavior. Ask yourself why there are brakes in a car. Is their function to slow the car down or to allow it to go fast? Boundary systems are like brakes on a car: without them, cars (or organizations) cannot operate at high speeds.

The concept of establishing negative boundaries is not unique to business. Consider the Ten Commandments from the Old Testament. They provide boundaries for Christian and Jewish life:

1. You shall have no other gods.
2. You shall not make any graven images and bow down.
3. You shall not take the name of the Lord in vain.
4. Keep the Sabbath holy—You shall do no work on that day.
5. Honor your father and mother.
6. You shall not kill.
7. You shall not commit adultery.
8. You shall not steal.
9. You shall not bear false witness against your neighbor.
10. You shall not covet anything that is your neighbor's.

These rules establish clear limits on behavior. Moreover, nine of the ten are stated in proscriptive terms.[7]

Figure 3.3 illustrates how a beliefs system and related boundary system work in tandem. The beliefs system provides organizational purpose and momentum to guide and motivate individual opportunity seeking within unlimited opportunity space. Within the beliefs system, boundary systems communicate the acceptable domain for search activity and thereby demarcate the opportunity domain as a subset of opportunity space within which organizational participants can exercise their energies. Beliefs systems and boundary systems transform unbounded opportunity space into a focused domain that organizational participants can be encouraged to exploit.

---

[7] I am grateful to Steven Perry, Harvard Business School class of 1990, who suggested this analogy during a class discussion of boundary systems.

Opportunity Space

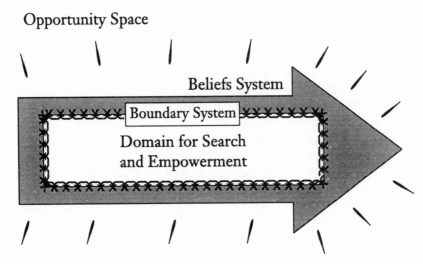

Figure 3.3   Transforming Opportunity Space into a Domain for Organizational Search

All systems that attempt to create accountability do so by delimiting organizational space for participants (Roberts and Scapens 1985). Beliefs about values and mission interact with rules and sanctions; commitment interacts with freedom within clearly stated boundaries. In business organizations, boundary systems are used to specify both means and ends. Formal systems establish two types of boundaries: business conduct boundaries and strategic boundaries. Both are determined through analysis of the risks associated with specific business strategies.

Business Conduct Boundaries

The most basic boundary systems are those that impose codes of business conduct. The standards encompassed in these codes have three sources: (1) society's laws, (2) the organization's beliefs systems, and (3) codes of behavior promulgated by industry and professional associations (Gatewood and Carroll 1991).

Like the Ten Commandments, codes of business conduct are stated for the most part in proscriptive terms. Proscribed behaviors typically include conflicts of interest, activities that contravene antitrust laws, actions that could compromise trade secrets or confidential information, the use of nonpublic information for stock trading, and certain types of payments to government officials.[8] These activities are ones that could jeopardize the well-being of an organization by exposing it to potential loss of assets, loss of reputation, or legal liability.

According to one recent survey, 77 percent of the companies with a net worth in excess of $100 million had formal codes of conduct, but only 48 percent of the firms with a net worth of $5 million to $100 million had explicit codes (Sweeney and Siers 1990). Why do some organizations have explicit codes and others do not? The answer, I believe, lies in the nature of the risks associated with specific business strategies.

Senior managers create business conduct boundaries when environmental uncertainty is high or internal trust is low.[9] Opportunity creates uncertainty. When unexpected situations arise, novel, untested organizational responses may be attempted. Faced with unusual opportunities, participants may, because of poor judgment or lack of relevant benchmarks, engage in conduct that senior managers would not condone. In a survey of profit-center managers, Merchant found that under conditions of high environmental uncertainty, managers were likely to manipulate profit figures (1990). As a result, in conditions of high environmental uncertainty, senior managers impose clear guidelines concerning unacceptable behavior (Perrow 1986, 21).

When trust is low in an organization because of a lack of shared experience or a high degree of heterogeneity among participants, or in loosely coupled organizations where shared values cannot be assumed, the risk of undesirable actions is exacerbated (Kanter 1977, 49–55). In these situations, the absence of shared commitment to the organization's mission and goals may result in self-interested behavior overriding organizational interests.

Commodity markets provide an extreme example of such a situation. Uncertainty is high and organizational trust is low due to the self-interested behavior of quasi-independent brokers. In a study of the adoption of working rules at the Chicago Board of Trade, Leblebici and Salancik (1982) noted that environmental uncertainty (price volatility) correlated strongly with the adoption of rules to govern

---

[8]For a prescriptive list of the areas that should be enumerated in a code of business conduct, see Baruch (1980).

[9]I thank Rosabeth Moss Kanter for pointing out the role of trust in relation to business conduct boundaries.

transactions. The number of rules increased as environmental uncertainty increased. Moreover, the number of sanctions imposed for violating these rules correlated with market volatility.

Unfortunately, improper conduct often occurs because managers misconstrue or rationalize their aberrant behavior. Gellerman (1986) lists four common rationalizations: (1) the action is not "really" wrong, (2) the action is in the organization's best interest, (3) the likelihood of being caught is small, and (4) if exposed, senior management would condone the behavior and protect the managers involved. However, businesses whose franchises rest on a reputation for integrity cannot risk employees misconstruing management's desires for performance as a mandate to engage in unethical or illegal behavior. Public accounting firms, legal firms, strategy consulting firms, investment banks, defense contractors, and pharmaceutical companies rely on trust to secure business.[10] These firms invariably establish clear business conduct boundaries.

One well-known investment bank, for example, states as part of its business principles, "Our assets are people, capital, and reputation. If any of these are lost, the last is the most difficult to regain." Business conduct boundaries in this firm preclude individuals from developing client relationships in undesirable industries, such as casinos and gambling companies, or from acting as a dealer-manager in unfriendly takeovers. The "do's and don'ts" manual of a large strategy consulting firm states that its consultants must not reveal the names of clients to anyone, including spouses, not employed by the firm and must not misrepresent themselves when attempting to gather competitive information for clients.

Unfortunately, senior managers often do not recognize the economic or strategic benefits of establishing business conduct boundaries. Even when they do, the benefits are difficult to estimate because they represent avoided costs. Most business conduct boundaries, then, are developed and communicated after an incident or crisis exposes the firm to unexpected asset or reputation losses. As Andrews (1989) has noted, businesses institute codes of conduct after a public scandal or an internal investigation of questionable behavior. General

---

[10] Trust, by definition, allows the "trustee" to engage in an action that would not otherwise be possible. The "trustor" voluntarily places resources at the disposal of the trustee with the understanding that based on future actions of the trustee, the trustor will be better off. This understanding will prove to be true only if the trustee is in fact trustworthy (Coleman 1990, 97–98).

Electric, for example, instituted a code of business conduct after two lower-level employees in its defense business misallocated project accounting costs, which caused the U.S. government to suspend the company as a supplier.[11]

Learning about an incident or crisis in another firm is a vicarious way of estimating the benefits of boundary systems. Not long ago, the business press reported that Wall Street investment firms were installing business conduct boundary systems as the result of a scandal involving the improper behavior of a few employees at Salomon Brothers, which severely damaged the business.[12] As Arrow reminds us,

The opportunity benefit, that is the change in benefits due to a change in action, may rise because of a decrease in the return to the present, unexamined action. In plain language, we have a "crisis." In William James's term, a "coercive fact" may be more persuasive than any speculation about potential benefits from change. The sinking of the *Titanic* led to iceberg patrols. (1974, 52)

Because managers often develop boundary systems in response to discrete incidents, the systems tend to be quite specific in their proscriptions and sanctions. General Electric, for example, issued a formal policy forbidding accounting allocations that would contravene government cost-accounting policies. Over time, a series of boundary systems builds up as organizations learn what types of behavior must be discouraged.

A special case arises when the reputation loss of one firm affects the reputation of other firms in the industry. Accounting firms, for example, have exclusive rights to conduct independent financial audits, but these rights can be withdrawn through political process. They are based on public trust in the ability of the firms to implement and police adequate standards for audits. The failure of one firm to live up to these standards can jeopardize the reputation and rules of competition for the entire profession.

For this reason, industry associations typically promulgate and enforce business conduct boundaries. These boundaries are codified through statements of professional conduct, and they are policed

---

[11]"U.S. Removes Most of Ban on Contracts with GE After Firm Agrees to Changes," *The Wall Street Journal*, 19 April 1985.

[12]See, for example, "On Wall Street, New Stress on Morality," *New York Times*, 11 September 1991; "Compliance Officers' Day in the Sun," *New York Times*, 20 October 1991.

and enforced through peer reviews and procedures for disciplinary action.[13] An extract from "Standards of Ethical Conduct for Management Accountants" (Institute of Management Accountants, 1983) serves as an example.

Management accountants have a responsibility to:

- Avoid actual or apparent conflicts of interest and advise all appropriate parties of any potential conflict.
- Refrain from engaging in any activity that would prejudice their ability to carry out their duties ethically.
- Refuse any gift, favor, or hospitality that would influence or would appear to influence their actions.
- Refrain from either actively or passively subverting the attainment of the organization's legitimate and ethical objective.
- Recognize and communicate professional limitations or other constraints that would preclude responsible judgment or successful performance of an activity.
- Communicate unfavorable as well as favorable information and professional judgments or opinions.
- Refrain from engaging in or supporting any activity that would discredit the profession.

Industry associations enforce codes of business conduct through specific sanctions. A review of 180 charges investigated between 1987 and 1990 by the Professional Conduct Committee of the Institute of Chartered Accountants of Ontario revealed that forty-one members of the institute were charged with violating fifteen different rules. Twenty percent of the charges dealt with rules designed to protect the "good reputation of the profession"; violations of rules dealing with "integrity" ranked second (16 percent). All forty-one people were convicted and suffered disciplinary actions including fines, mandated remedial education, and, in some cases, suspension (Brooks and Fortunato 1991).

Franchisors and corporate headquarters of dispersed retail businesses also formalize and enforce business conduct boundaries when the reputation loss of one branch is likely to adversely affect other branches in the system. Because retail franchises and multiple-branch businesses, such as McDonald's, Marriott Hotels, Wal-Mart, Nord-

---

[13] The interested reader can refer to Gorlin (1986) to examine the "shall nots" contained in the codes of professional conduct for accountants, architects, bankers, engineers, insurance agents, and real-estate agents, who frequently organize as profit-making firms.

strom, and Pepsi Bottlers, compete by offering consistency in products and service, a failure in any one branch adversely affects all branches in the system. Roy Rogers Restaurants, for example, imposes stringent terms on their independent franchise operators. Constraints on training, quality standards, cleanliness, and menu specifications are detailed and strictly enforced (Bruns and Murray 1989).

Performance pressures also influence the imposition of formal business conduct boundaries. In a survey of 590 firms, Rich, Smith, and Mihalek (1990) found that pressure to achieve specific net income or ROI targets was strongest in firms with formal codes of business conduct. The authors had hypothesized there would be less pressure to achieve financial targets and manipulate earnings if a company had a formal code of conduct. However, causality is more likely in the opposite direction. Performance pressures create a need for codes of conduct. Carroll's survey of 238 managers suggests that a majority of managers feel pressure at some time to compromise personal standards to achieve company goals (1975, 77). As noted earlier, Merchant also found that pressure to meet financial targets resulted in increased incidence of managers manipulating accounting performance measures. Firms that use diagnostic control systems (discussed in the next chapter) to pressure employees must create strict guidelines to make it clear that certain undesirable behaviors will not be tolerated.

Codes of business conduct inevitably limit freedom of action. While some organizational participants may not want to be constrained by such rules, many participants actually want to have codes of conduct in place and enforceable. When codes of conduct align with personal standards of conduct, there will be little cause for resentment. According to a majority of respondents to a *Harvard Business Review* survey, these codes can serve as a defense against inappropriate pressure from immediate superiors to engage in conduct that violates personal standards (Brenner and Molander 1977). Thus, codes of business conduct can be liberating for lower- and middle-level managers.[14]

Strategic Boundaries

Strategic boundaries focus on opportunity-seeking behavior to support explicit organizational strategies. Although strategic planning

[14] I thank the members of the Harvard Business School seminar "Decision Making and Ethical Values" for this observation.

systems serve several different purposes, a principal purpose is to limit search activities. Strategic planning is often used to stipulate what search activities are not acceptable and should not be pursued.

Business opportunities emerge rapidly and erratically, but attempts to specify how a business will compete can be counterproductive to success. Senior managers can, however, specify the range of business opportunities in which they do not want the organization to expend resources. To do so, these managers use planning tools and checklists. A large computer company, for example, uses its strategic planning process to segregate its opportunity set into what managers call "green space" and "red space." Green space is the acceptable domain for opportunity-seeking. Red space represents products and markets in which individuals are precluded from searching for new opportunities, even though the organization could compete in these areas. A British charity uses a similar system to monitor strategic boundaries. It maintains a "gray list" of companies deemed to be undesirable and whose contributions it will neither solicit nor accept.

Just as business conduct boundaries are usually imposed after an incident or crisis, strategic boundaries are usually imposed when excessive search behavior and experimentation have risked dissipating the firm's resources. Managers want to motivate creative search behavior, but unfocused search can waste financial capital and management attention. Harold Geneen, the legendary chief executive of ITT, described just such a situation and his decision to implement strategic boundaries:

The road you don't take can be as important in your life as the one you do take. In the very early sixties, when computers were seen as the wave of the future, many of our engineers, particularly those in Europe, were eager to surge into this new, phenomenal field. Our German company, which was far ahead of the others in computer development, outbid IBM and won a contract to build a computerized reservation system for Air France. We lost $10 million on that contract. I called a halt to further computer development.

I withstood a great deal of pressure at the time to enforce my early prohibition against the development of general-purpose computers at ITT. Not only our engineers but our investment advisers favored computer development. Everyone who could was going into computers, they said. The mere announcement would send our stock up, they promised. I stood firm. (1984, 219–20)

In an attempt to stem Chrysler's losses in the mid- to late-1970s, John Riccardo and, later, Lee Iacocca established strategic boundaries to stop the unproductive use of resources in multiple markets. To refocus the business on North American auto and truck production, strategic boundaries were established to place European, African, and all nonautomobile businesses outside the opportunity set of the business. As a result, the international and tank businesses were sold off, and Chrysler exited leasing (Iacocca 1984, 165, 187–88).

In addition to specifying the opportunities to be avoided, strategic boundaries can set limits for acceptable opportunities. These opportunities can then be ranked. Exhibit 3.2 presents the strategic checklist used by Automatic Data Processing to guide its annual strategic planning exercise.

The seven requirements on the list represent *minimum* tests that must be passed for a business to be funded or acquired by ADP. ADP managers consider those criteria preceded by two dots to be especially important. While passing a test is necessary, it does not guarantee acquisition: further analysis must then be carried out to ascertain if a business would be a suitable acquisition candidate. Failing any of the tests, however, is sufficient for rejecting the business.

Strategic boundaries like ADP's checklist can force subordinate managers to consider exiting undesirable businesses. Using this list as a catalyst, for example, ADP decided to sell its highly profitable Electronic Financial Services business before competitive conditions impaired its value. A review of the business against the list suggested that the business was drifting outside the strategic boundaries. Competition from Mastercard and VISA, coupled with changing dynamics in the banking industry, tripped several critical boundary conditions (Simons and Weston 1989). ADP has long used this strategic boundary system to prune businesses, which may help to explain how it has achieved the longest unbroken record of double-digit quarterly earnings-per-share increases of any U.S. public company (128 consecutive quarters—32 years—at last count).[15]

The boundaries do not have to be as specific as ADP's. Any observer of American business will be familiar with the strategic boundary repeated so often by John Welch, Jr., chairman of General Electric: GE will exit any business in which it cannot achieve a number one or number two market position.

A second common strategic boundary system in many organizations is the asset acquisition system (capital budgeting system). In

[15] *Forbes* (4 January 1993): 99; *Fortune*, 20 September 1993: 80.

Seven Key Requirements for Pursuing Major Service Businesses and Products (*Most* must be satisfied to have a good strategy. A poor strategy can seldom succeed, even with excellent execution.)

(1) *Revenue Potential*   Over $50 million of annual *recurring* revenue for an SBU, $20 million for a line of business, and $5 million for a product.

(2) *Growth Potential*   At least a continuing 15% growth rate, preferably over 20%, with good probability (and plans). (This might be less for defensive positions in *existing* business or where ROI is very high.)

(3) *Desirable Competitive Position*
    a. Fragmented current market (exclusive of ADP's position).
    b. ADP in #1 or 2 position (or #3, if fragmented market) with potential to be #1 within five years.
    c. There is no major (deep pockets) illogical players (usually zero profit objectives) whose pricing would likely undermine our profitability.

(4) *Products: Standardized Computer-Related Business Applications (Front and Back Office)*
    a.. Mass-marketable (noncustomized potential for large number of prospects/transactions).
    b.. Mass-producible (noncustomized, near-level production for large number of transactions with limited labor).
    c.. Consistently superior direct client service features and performance, with clear client accountability (see Exhibit B).
    d. Extendable to additional integratable applications, particularly in front-office.
    e.. Influenced by a standardizing "Third Force" (viz—regulations, licensors, peers).
    f. Supported/recommended by influential third forces (viz—banks, CPAs, peers, hardware partners, licensors, trade associations).
    g. Leverages existing client/marketplace relationships (concentric circles).
    h.. Different from competition in noticeable/valuable sustainable ways (UCP/USP) that are not solely dependent upon automation and technology.

(5) *Sustainability of Acceptable Growth in the Market*   Particularly critical for new, nonadjacent business, to earn steady growth and premium pricing.
    a.. Very distinctive product/service position (see Exhibit A).
    b.. Potential and plans for significant client accretion.
    c. Good client life cycle and/or exit barriers. (*Do* consider long-term lock-ins!)
    d. Entry barriers to strong competition. (Long-term client contracts may be relevant.)
    e.. High *net* $ value-added for client (i.e.—client benefit vs. ADP charges) vs. client's other alternatives (see Exhibit A).

    f.   Stable client preferences and habits (vs. fickle consumer types).

    g. Lowest cost producer. (Not lowest price seller.)

(6) *Strong Management* Experience, commitment, focus, capability, credibility, conformity to Key Factors to Success (Exhibit B).

(7) *Promising Financial Potential*

    a.. High-confidence business plan (good trends in margins, growth, lifecycles, ROA).

    b. High confidence risk/reward relationship (no single client dependency).

    c. High product frequency of use/repetitive revenue (stability/predictability).

    d. Clear development checkpoints/contingency plans (and aborts, if warranted).

    e.. Feasible exit plan and absorbable exit cost (if needed).

    f.. Acceptable prospective return (ROI) on prospective investments (including Bow Waves, *all* capital investments, future acquisitions, and cost of money).

    g. Keep client-site hardware off balance sheet, if feasible.

    h. NBE% should seldom exceed processing margin, except where there is a very long client lifecycle . . . in order to provide an adequate return for the risk/difficulty and $ of NBE investment.

Source: Robert Simons and Hilary Weston, Automatic Data Processing: The EFS Decision, case 9-190-059. Boston: Harvard Business School, 1989. Reprinted by permission.

Exhibit 3.2 ADP's Strategic Checklist

the most basic sense, virtually all asset acquisition systems specify a minimum rate of return or discount rate that should be used by individuals when proposing asset acquisitions. Because senior management cannot foresee all the opportunities available to the firm, senior managers reviewing asset acquisition proposals set a lower limit on acceptable proposals and motivate organizational participants to search for the best possible asset utilization opportunities within the boundary conditions. The effect is to say, "I will not tell you what opportunities to sponsor. Find the best opportunities out there and present them to us, but do not consider proposals with an ROI less than 15 percent." The hurdle rate sets minimum boundaries.

Boundary System Incentives

Because attention is limited, individuals will attend to specific systems only if there is some inducement to do so, but how should managers reward subordinates for not breaking the rules?

Managers have little reason to reward employees for not violating stated boundaries. If boundaries are clear and communicated effectively, most organizational participants will not contravene stated policies. To reward 99 percent of an organization's participants for conformance with business conduct boundaries, for example, would incur high costs without any increase in organizational performance. Therefore, boundary system incentives are usually punitive sanctions. While some authors, for example, Gatewood and Carroll (1991), have called for new measurement and control systems to monitor ethical behavior and reward those who act ethically, few organizations have followed these prescriptions. Instead, most organizations punish individuals who act in defiance of stated policies or accepted standards of behavior.

Like other norms of behavior, boundary systems cannot be effective without credible sanctions (Coleman 1990, chs. 10, 11). Seventy percent of companies surveyed by Sweeney and Siers (1990) included explicit sanctions and disciplinary measures in their codes of conduct. As John Vogel, the legal counsel responsible for implementing General Electric's compliance program commented in a 1989 address to Harvard Business School students, "When it comes to compliance with standards of business conduct, there are no carrots—only sticks."

Sanctions are also the principal means of enforcement for strategic boundaries. Harold Geneen describes how he enforced his decision to stop dissipating resources on general purpose computer projects:

Others continued to work on computer development for us on the sly. When I learned of this, I hired two very competent engineers and gave them a special assignment which lasted for several years; to roam at will through all our worldwide engineering and new products laboratories and to root out, stamp out, and stop all incipient general-purpose computer projects by whatever code name they were called; and if they were given any trouble, to call us at headquarters and we would stamp them out for them. (1984, 220)

For sanctions to be effective, threats must be clear and credible. Therefore, managers use a "no exceptions" policy to send unambiguous signals that transgressors will be punished. In all competitive businesses, setting difficult targets and linking rewards with performance create pressures for people to act in ways that superiors would deem inappropriate. Boundary systems warn that some types of behavior or activity will not be tolerated.

Boundary Systems and Organizational Freedom

Organizational participants can view boundary systems as either constraining or liberating. An earlier example showed how codes of conduct can constrain unethical behavior. Usually, however, participants find rules of unacceptable behavior allow freedom of action within specified bounds. Wilfred Brown, the president of a British industrial firm, maintains that a lack of rules can be deceiving. At first, subordinates believe they have freedom of action, but they quickly learn that superiors hold them accountable to unwritten rules that can only be determined through trial and error. The result is uncertainty and a reluctance to act.

I have found, however, particularly in discussing jobs with external applicants, that the array of policy represented by our Policy Document, Standing Orders and Directives, causes people to assume the precise opposite of the real situation, i.e., that the extant written policy will deprive them of the right to make decisions. In fact, it is only by delineating the area of "freedom" in this way that a subordinate knows when he can make decisions. The absence of written policy leaves him in a position where any decision he takes, however apparently trivial, may infringe upon an unstated policy and produce a reprimand. (Brown 1960, 97–98, cited in Perrow 1986, 21–22)

In discussing the value of rules, Perrow summarizes:

Rules protect those who are subject to them. Rules are means of preserving group autonomy and freedom; to reduce the number of rules in an organization generally means to make it more impersonal, more inflexible, more standardized. But even given this, rules are still a bore. We would all prefer to be free of them, or so it would seem. Actually, only *some* rules are bores. The good, effective rules are rarely noticed; the bad ones stand out. (p. 24)

In a perverse way, constraint creates the freedom in which the inspirational role of beliefs systems can flourish. It is the tension created by the pairing of beliefs and boundaries that allows commitment, empowerment, and freedom to contribute.

Risks in Using Boundary Systems to Set Strategic Domains

There is always the risk that boundaries—especially strategic ones—may be misspecified. Organizations and their environments often change faster than organizational rules (Perrow 1986, 26). Wang Computer, for example, built a strong market franchise in the desktop word-processing industry by following a simple strategic boundary: it would not compete in any market segment in which IBM was active. This strategic boundary allowed Wang to build a profitable niche in the desktop word-processing industry. Unfortunately, when technology shifted to allow personal computers to host word-processing software, this strategic boundary contributed to the company's rapid deterioration.[16] We might also ask what opportunities ITT passed up in terms of the later integration of telecommunications and computers.

If improperly set, strategic boundaries can hinder adaptation to changing product, market, technological, and environmental conditions. Boundary systems make it risky for employees to search for new opportunities outside acceptable domains of activity. Rigid strategic boundaries make it clear to employees that using company resources to experiment in proscribed product markets is subject to discovery and punishment.

By not allowing opportunity-seeking behavior in specified product markets, senior managers may preclude the organization from acquiring an early advantage in new and unanticipated ventures. Levitt's famous article "Marketing Myopia" (1960) describes numerous instances of companies and industries that have declined as a result of management's failure to anticipate the changing nature of strategic domains, and other examples abound. As Levitt states, "Today's growth industry is tomorrow's buggy whip." Senior managers must be flexible and redefine strategic boundaries as conditions change.

A similar risk exists for other types of boundary systems. Asset acquisition systems may constrain a firm's opportunities by inhibiting the submission of strategically important projects that show poor short-term returns. Some capital projects offer little immediate financial return but may enhance the organization's capabilities to adapt or enter new product markets over time. Allowing asset acquisition systems to constrain search can be fatal to long-term competitiveness (Baldwin and Clark 1992; Porter 1992). On the other hand, guidelines perceived as unreasonably constraining may cause participants to

---

[16]From "The Doctor Draws the Boundaries: A Study of Boundary Systems at Wang Laboratories," a paper prepared by W. Herkenham for the Harvard Business School MBA course Strategic Management Systems, 1989.

"massage" assumptions and estimates so that boundary conditions are not tripped.

Actions Speak Louder Than Words

Beliefs and boundaries are the formal, explicit statements of the core beliefs and values of senior management. We must recognize, however, the distinction between espoused theories and theories-in-use (Argyris and Schön 1978, 10–11). The former is what we say; the latter is what we do. Espoused beliefs and boundaries may be ineffective if they are inconsistent with actions that have been established through tradition and implicitly sanctioned by senior management. If employees know that managers routinely bribe government officials to speed the passage of paper work, proscription is unenforceable. The horrific nuclear accident at Chernobyl provides a glimpse into potential consequences.

The attitude at the top naturally affected attitudes lower down in the hierarchy. Zhores Medvedev quotes one of the day-shift operators at Chernobyl who explained that, under the same circumstances, he too might have violated regulations, as the night-shift operator had done:

> Why? let me try to explain. . . . Firstly, we often don't see the need to observe our laws to the letter because these laws are broken all around us before our eyes—and quite often! . . . Can it really be the Government Commission that accepted block 4 as ready for operation did not know that it was accepting it incomplete? Of course they knew. . . . (Holloway 1990, 5)

The actions of superiors (theories-in-use) may override the espoused beliefs and boundaries established to protect the integrity of the organization.

Beliefs, Boundaries, and Managers

The primary responsibilities of senior management are to state the core values and vision for the organization, analyze business risks, and delimit appropriate arenas for competition. In their study of decision making by senior managers, Donaldson and Lorsch concluded:

Central to each belief system is management's vision of the company's distinctive competence. In its managers' minds, this vision defines what the company's economic, human, and technical resources can—and cannot—accomplish: the kinds of economic activity the firm should undertake and how this activity is to be conducted. In essence, therefore, it shapes the strategic means they select. . . . Thus management's subjective beliefs about individual competence and comparative advantage lie behind the objective realities of the firm's economic and financial environment. (1983, 80)

Although senior managers usually draft beliefs statements themselves, they may circulate drafts to a small group of colleagues for comment and refinement. Circulation ensures the clear and concise communication of their vision to the organization. Usually senior managers also initiate strategic boundaries.

In most routine cases, senior managers delegate the promulgation of business conduct codes to staff professionals. However, senior managers review and approve important business conduct boundaries. In a recent survey, codes of conduct were approved by the CEO or at the board of directors level for 95 percent of companies sampled (Sweeney and Siers 1990).

Effective senior managers signal the importance of formal beliefs systems through such actions as speeches, award presentations, and group meetings (Kotter 1990, ch. 5). Through their public words and actions, senior managers make it clear that boundaries are to be respected. In 75 percent of firms sampled by Sweeney and Siers compliance failures were reported to the CEO and the board. According to Andrews (1989), senior managers mete out punishments personally.

Beliefs, Boundaries, and Control
Staff Specialists

The role of control staff specialists—accountants, quality controllers, internal auditors, and information technology experts—varies for different types of management control systems. For some systems, staff specialists act as key designers and information gatekeepers; for other systems, staff experts act primarily as facilitators (Simons 1987b, 1990).

Control staff specialists play two important roles in beliefs systems and boundary systems. First, they maintain these systems. Maintenance activities include disseminating materials in support of beliefs systems, conducting surveys to measure employee awareness, designing education seminars, communicating and updating codes of business conduct, preparing strategic checklists, and preparing capital acquisition guidelines. Second, control staff specialists police boundaries. Internal auditors, budget analysts, and planners are alert for evidence that individuals are engaged in activities that contravene management intentions and policies. Staff specialists check business plans and capital acquisition proposals to ensure that proposals do not take the business into areas outside specified boundaries.

Summary

This chapter is about information, symbols, and rules communicated and reinforced systematically. In many respects, these ideas are compatible with notions of organizational culture. Indeed, many anthropologists and sociologists define culture as the set of rules and standards that state what people in organizations should and should not do (Schall 1983). Cultural rules are often explicit: failure to abide by the rules results in sanction. Moreover, rules and symbols take on a life of their own as they create new meaning for organizational participants (Dent 1991; Feldman and March 1981). Beliefs systems create norms and serve as cultural ideals. The rules embodied in boundary systems both create and are created by the culture of an organization.

Beliefs systems and boundary systems are the formal, information-based routines and procedures that managers use to maintain or alter patterns in organizational activities. Senior managers and control specialists transform these static documents and procedures into systems by communicating information about beliefs and boundaries throughout the organization through education programs, documents, awareness surveys, and feedback sessions. Beliefs and boundaries, if they are to be living systems, must be reinforced continually within the organization.

Working together, these two levers create forces of yin and yang. The warm, positive, inspirational beliefs are a foil to dark, cold constraints. The result is a dynamic tension between commitment and punishment. Senior managers drive both processes.

Leadership should protect against organizational drift and misguided behaviors by establishing direction, aligning, motivating, and inspiring people, and defending institutional integrity (Selznick 1957,

62–64). Management control systems transform unbounded opportunity space into a focused domain that organizational participants are encouraged to exploit. Two key variables—core values and business risks—must be analyzed to understand how these systems can be designed and used to support business strategy.

Beliefs and boundaries are essential to organizational life. As opportunities expand and the pressures for performance increase, a clear beliefs system and enforceable boundary system become increasingly important. In addition to providing momentum and commitment, a strong beliefs system and clear boundaries assure managers that subordinates are not engaging in activities that could jeopardize the integrity of the business and are not dissipating organizational resources through projects or actions that do not build on competitive strengths. This assurance allows managers to concentrate on positioning their firms to meet the competitive challenges of the marketplace.

CHAPTER 4

Diagnostic Control Systems: Implementing Intended Strategies

This chapter introduces the third lever of control: diagnostic control systems. These feedback systems, which are the backbone of traditional management control, are designed to ensure predictable goal achievement. Curiously, what is powerful (and potentially dangerous) about these systems is the fact that managers pay little attention to them.

In organizations of any size, the complexity of operations and the sheer number of decisions needed daily force subordinates to make many decisions on their own. At the same time, senior managers need assurance that these decisions are in line with organizational goals. Diagnostic control systems are the formal information systems that managers use to monitor organizational outcomes and correct deviations from preset standards of performance.

Three features distinguish diagnostic control systems: (1) the ability to measure the outputs of a process, (2) the existence of predetermined standards against which actual results can be compared, and (3) the ability to correct deviations from standards. Figure 4.1 illustrates the generic features of all diagnostic control systems.

Most discussions of control systems have highlighted the importance of monitoring results of lower-level decisions and activities and have labeled this type of *ex post* monitoring "output control," "performance control," or "results control" (Ouchi 1977; Mintzberg 1979,

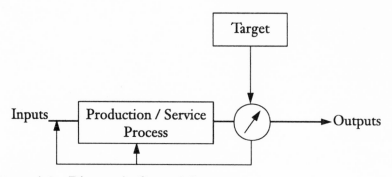

Figure 4.1   Diagnostic Control Systems

149; Merchant 1985, ch. 2). A doctor's physical examination is a type of *ex post* monitoring: blood pressure, heart rhythms, cholesterol levels, and other variables are measured and compared against standards established for the patient's sex, weight, and age. Deviations are noted, and corrective treatment is prescribed.

The underlying phenomenon is the same for control of an individual, a machine, a department, or a production line. Inputs—labor, information, material, energy, and so forth—are fed into a production or service process that transforms them into outputs of value. The quantity and quality of outputs are measured periodically and compared against preset standards. Feedback of variance information allows adjustment of inputs or fine tuning of the process so that future outputs will more closely match preset standards. From time to time, based on consistent discrepancies—for example, consistently higher outputs than anticipated—preset standards are adjusted.

Based on this depiction, it is not surprising that the thermostat in a home is another popular analogy for a diagnostic control system. The thermostat regulates air temperature by turning a furnace on and off, based on continual comparisons of actual air temperature with a preset standard (Lawler and Rhode 1976, 40–41). The gauges in the cockpit of an airplane serve a diagnostic control function, feeding variance information to the pilot who continually scans for signs of abnormal functioning and adjusts airplane controls to keep critical variables within preset limits.

Virtually all writing on management control systems refers to diagnostic control systems. In fact, the term *management control* is usually synonymous with the definition of diagnostic control pre-

Goals and objectives systems
Business plans
Profit plans and budgets
Expense center budgets
Project monitoring systems
Brand revenue/market share monitoring systems
Human resource plans
Standard cost accounting systems
Management-by-objectives systems

Exhibit 4.1 Typical Diagnostic Control Systems

sented here. Merchant, for example, states, "Control, which essentially means 'keeping things on track', ranks as one of the critical functions of management. . . . Good control means that an informed person can be reasonably confident that no major, unpleasant surprises will occur" (1985, 1, 10). Lorange and Scott Morton adopt a similar position:

The *fundamental purpose* for management control systems is to help management accomplish an organization's objectives by providing a formalized framework for (1) the identification of pertinent control variables, (2) the development of good short-term plans, (3) the recording of the degree of actual fulfillment of short-term plans along the set of control variables, and (4) the diagnosis of deviations. (1974, 41–42)

Profit plans and budgets are the most pervasive diagnostic control systems in modern business firms. In a survey of 402 U.S. firms, 97 percent reported using a formal budgeting program in their business (Umapathy 1987, 18). Exhibit 4.1 provides a list of other diagnostic control systems typically found in business organizations.

Alternatives to Diagnostic Control

All organizational processes can be decomposed into inputs—labor, capital, information, energy, materials, and so forth—that are transformed into outputs of value. While diagnostic controls measure and monitor outputs, in certain circumstances managers may choose to control the inputs or the process that creates outputs directly. If no variation in the transformation process is desired, standard operating procedures can specify how every action should be performed. Control is then achieved by telling people how to do their jobs and ensuring that they follow instructions. This is Frederick Taylor's approach, discussed in Chapter 2. Efficiency studies, internal control standards, and desired quality or safety levels are used to develop detailed operating procedures. Standard operating procedures are used when standardization achieves efficiencies, as it does on an assembly line; when the risk of theft of valuable assets is high as it is in a casino; or when quality and safety are essential to product performance, as it is in the operation of a nuclear power plant.

In each of these cases, standardization is designed to minimize individual creativity and resultant error. For certain tasks, creativity brings the risks of inefficiency, theft, and quality or safety failures: new assembly-line employees must learn how to balance the line; novel ways of dealing cards and handling cash may circumvent existing casino controls; experiments in operating procedures may fail to anticipate quality or system failure problems. After all, how much creativity do we want from employees who are operating a nuclear power plant?

Alternatively, managers can control outputs through the careful selection of inputs. Selecting fine diamonds ensures a high-quality ring. Carefully selecting and training individual workers can provide assurance that tasks will be performed in the desired way. In rare situations in which it is impossible to monitor either the work process or the outputs directly, selection and training of workers are the only viable means of control. In these circumstances, however, the selection of new recruits and the indoctrination of organizational mission, goals, and work methods consumes much of the organization's energy. This approach is used in training individuals who must work alone in remote locations, for example, Jesuit missionaries and United States Forest Rangers (Kaufman 1960). For most business organizations, however, input controls alone rarely ensure that tasks are done as management intended. Furthermore, the intensive training and indoctrination necessary for this type of input control are too costly for most businesses.

In business organizations, then, neither input controls nor process standardization are viable alternatives for diagnostic management controls. Standardization drives out creativity and the potential for innovation. Input controls allow maximum creativity but are too costly and carry the risk that organizational goals will be subordinated to individual self-interest. Diagnostic control systems offer the appropriate middle ground for managers.

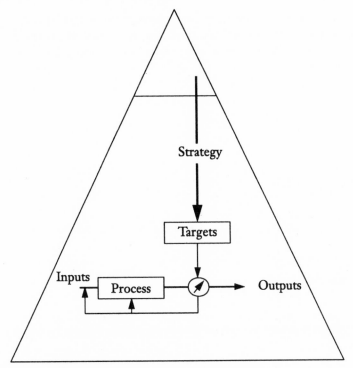

Figure 4.2   Using Diagnostic Control Systems to
Implement Strategy

Intended Strategy and Critical
Performance Variables

The targets embedded in the formal plans and programs of
intended strategies are used to monitor organizational compliance to
the strategies. Diagnostic control systems, which monitor organizational outcomes, are, therefore, essential levers for implementing intended strategies (Figure 4.2).

Diagnostic control systems attempt to measure output variables
that represent important performance dimensions of a given strategy.
I shall call these output variables *critical performance variables*. Others
have used such terms as "key success factors" and "critical success
factors." In this book, critical performance variables are those factors
that must be achieved or implemented successfully for the intended
strategy of the business to succeed. One way to uncover these variables is to imagine that a strategy failed and then ask what factors
would be identified as causes for this failure.

Critical performance variables either influence the probability of successfully meeting goals (an effectiveness criterion) or provide the largest potential for marginal gain over time (an efficiency criterion). Thus, effectiveness and efficiency are the prime criteria for the selection of measures used in diagnostic control systems (Anthony 1988, 34).

Past and Current Practice

The first systematic identification of critical performance variables is attributed to Donaldson Brown, who developed his techniques as chief financial officer at Dupont about 1915 and later introduced the techniques to General Motors (Kuhn 1986, 58–62; Johnson and Kaplan 1987, 86, 101). As shown in Figure 4.3, Brown's formulation disaggregated return-on-investment to encompass a series of financial indicators that were related to asset turnover and profitability on sales. These critical performance variables were financial in nature, but

Brown naturally realized that the success of GM often hinged on its ability to control nonfinancial variables. He mentioned the importance of manufacturing, advertising, and marketing. He added that producing an article "exclusive in design, possessing superior engineering qualities and carrying with it a peculiar appeal to fashion" afforded the opportunity for a favorable rate of return. Hence risk could be minimized through "skill in progressive engineering improvements" and "ingenuity in anticipating the changing tastes of the buying public."

So to control performance the firm often had to adjust in ways that were nonfinancial, though the results of the adaptation were ultimately reflected in the financial rate-of-return measure and in the underlying critical financial variables. That is, nonfinancial variables could be mapped onto the more critical financial variables so as to inform the designers and decision makers what performance improvements for the stockholders might be expected. (Kuhn 1986, 61)

By the 1960s the concept of critical performance variables had broadened to include a range of factors such as market pricing, new product introduction, customer service, and logistics (Daniel 1966). Today, customer satisfaction and quality are often cited as critical performance variables.

Consider, for example, Nordstrom, a specialty retailer that competes by offering high-value fashion clothing and exceptional customer service. Nordstrom relies on merchandise selection and the

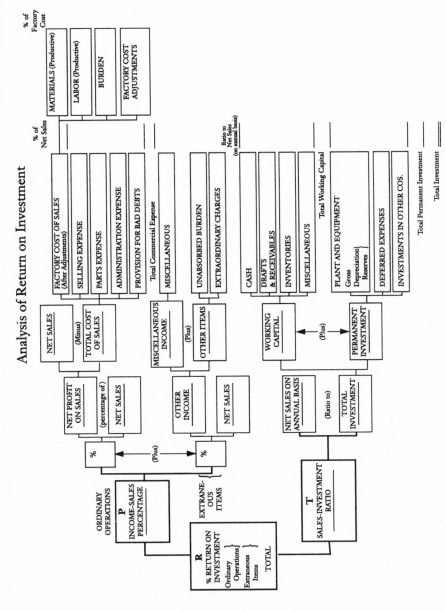

Figure 4.3 Brown's Return-on-Investment Form

SOURCE: Donaldson Brown, *Some Reminiscences of an Industrialist* (Easton, Penn.: Hive Publishing Company, 1977), 129.

personal attention of salespeople to win customers. The critical performance variables for this business are (1) customer loyalty and (2) entrepreneurial salespeople. Salespeople ("Nordies," as they are called) are encouraged to do whatever it takes to satisfy a customer. Thank you notes, home deliveries, and changing flat tires for customers are commonplace occurrences among Nordstrom salespeople. Customer loyalty is the desired outcome, and it is critical for the repeat business needed to support Nordstrom's inventory and pricing policies (Simons and Weston 1990c).

Once critical performance variables are determined, diagnostic control systems provide the indicators to ensure that they are managed effectively and efficiently. At Nordstrom, the most successful salespeople are those who treat customers as assets. These entrepreneurs creatively generate repeat business by alerting their customers to new merchandise and sending follow-up notes—much as a good car salesman or stockbroker might do. A key diagnostic measure, then, is sales-per-hour, which allows managers to know which salespeople have built a cadre of loyal customers and generated repeat business.

Figure 4.4 illustrates the relationship between business strategy, critical performance variables, and diagnostic control systems.

Determining Critical Performance Variables

To identify the correct critical performance variables it is necessary to analyze the firm's intended strategy and the specific goals associated with that strategy. Once critical performance variables are determined, measures can be developed. A low-cost strategy for a parts manufacturer that emphasizes volume, quality, and standardized products may require measures that focus on internal manufacturing efficiencies, quality improvement, market share, and delivery metrics. In contrast, a product innovation strategy for a medical supply company may stress measures such as time-to-market and percent-of-revenue from new products. But because measurement procedures are usually codified and delegated to staff specialists who are not business managers, these measures are rarely reviewed for relevance or robustness. Over time, strategies may change, which may change critical performance variables.

Different strategies call for different critical performance variables and different diagnostic control systems. In the late 1980s, IBM

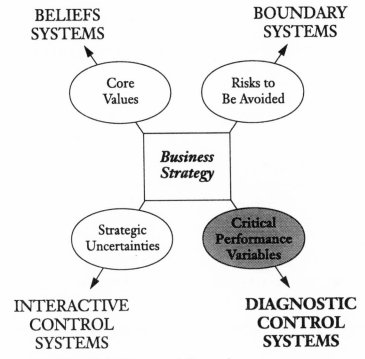

Figure 4.4   The Third Lever of Control

shifted from a product-driven strategy to a market-driven strategy. Under the old strategy, IBM had focused its marketing skills on selling proprietary technologies. Technology specialists developed new products and applications; the marketing and services division sold these products to customers. Headquarters knew which products were most profitable, which technologies should be promoted aggressively, and the capacity of their different production facilities. Because unit volumes and mix—"moving the boxes"—were critical performance variables, a diagnostic sales plan and quota system allocated production to individual branch offices and rewarded sales representatives for meeting or exceeding allocated product quotas. This approach worked well because the products were standardized and they could be marketed with little concern about different customer applications and end uses. Customers relied on in-house programmers and other software vendors to put IBM products to use.

By the mid-1980s, however, IBM customers began demanding complete solutions for their information needs, and IBM was forced to adopt a new strategy. The new, market-driven strategy pushed decision making down to the salespeople, who were closest to the customer. Rather than being told what to sell by headquarters, sales representatives worked with customers to tailor product offerings to meet customer needs. Under the new strategy, critical performance variables were revenue growth, market share, and ability to meet customer needs. The sales plan and quota system was abandoned in favor of a diagnostic control system that measured customer revenues and branch profits (Simons and Weston, 1990a).

Kaplan and Norton (1992) propose a systematic way of analyzing critical performance variables and measures associated with intended strategies. In their analysis, diagnostic control system measures are grouped into four categories: financial measures; customer measures; internal business measures; and innovation and learning measures. These categories make up what Kaplan and Norton term a "balanced scorecard." They argue that effective managers use diagnostic measures in each of these four categories simultaneously to guide their business toward desired goals. Figure 4.5 illustrates Kaplan and Norton's approach.

Examples of balanced scorecard measures are:

Financial Measures
    Cash flow
    Sales growth
    Operating income
    Return on equity
Customer Measures
    Percent of sales from new products
    On time delivery
    Share of important customers' purchases
    Ranking by important customers
Internal Business Measures
    Cycle time
    Unit cost
    Yield
    New product introductions
Innovation and Learning Measures
    Time to develop new generation of products
    Life cycle to product maturity
    Time to market versus competition

Diagnostic control systems are designed to trigger the adjust-

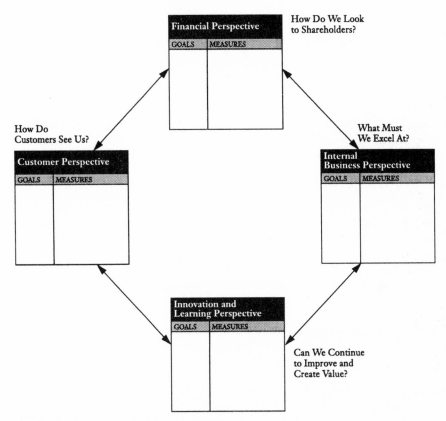

Figure 4.5 The Balanced Scorecard

SOURCE: Robert S. Kaplan and David P. Norton, "The Balanced Scorecard—Measures That Drive Performance," *Harvard Business Review* (January–February 1992). Reprinted by permission.

ment of the targets embedded in the plans and programs required for the implementation of intended strategies. Argyris and Schön have termed this single-loop learning.

> The organization's ability to remain stable in a changing context denotes a kind of learning . . . we call single-loop learning. There is a single feed-back loop which connects detected outcomes of action to organizational strategies and assumptions which are modified so as to keep organizational performance within the range set by organizational norms. The norms themselves—for product quality, sales, or task performance—remain unchanged. (1978, 18)

Diagnostic control systems can be used to set standards and measure outputs for individual managers or for parts of the business. However, setting goals and measuring the performance of managers raises issues of focus and motivation, while setting goals and measuring the performance of business units raises issues of resource allocation. Thus, critical performance variables depend on the level of analysis. A set of critical performance variables identified for monitoring the performance of a shift supervisor will be different from the set identified for monitoring the performance of the overall business.

Conserving Management Attention

Diagnostic control systems allow the organization to achieve goals without constant management oversight. Thus, these systems allow management-by-exception. Although virtually all writing on management control systems refers to diagnostic control systems, managers in fact spend little time directly involved with them. Recalling the thermostat analogy, once the desired temperature level is set, the system will self-regulate and require no further attention. Paying attention only to significant deviations is appropriate for a wide range of organizational activities and yields high ROM. Using management-by-exception allows managers to allocate attention effectively to monitor and control production processes, project milestones, personal goals, and plans and budgets.

From the perspective of organizational participants, diagnostic control systems allow maximum autonomy: individuals are held accountable for results but have the freedom to choose how to accomplish desired ends. They can use their imagination and effort to adjust inputs and processes as needed. In turn, managers can be confident that participants are working toward agreed goals—earnings targets, expense reductions, project milestones, market share increases— without constant monitoring. Feedback systems—based on goal-setting, measurement, and rewards—ensure that participants are working in the right direction and allow managers to dispense with constant surveillance.

For this to occur, however, managers invest their attention in diagnostic control systems in three instances.

1. *Setting and negotiating goals.* To ensure the achievement of business strategies, managers must personally negotiate performance goals with subordinates. Managers must decide on appropriate goals

and their level of difficulty. They must also structure rewards and incentives related to achievement. Managers do not delegate periodic goal setting because these goals are vital to the achievement of strategy. The goal-setting process, however, can be restricted to short periods of management attention. In 93 percent of the American firms surveyed by Umapathy, budget goals were established only once during each annual (or longer) cycle (1987, 84).

2. *Receiving updates and exception reports.* Managers must use monthly and quarterly updates and exception reports as their principal diagnostic tools. Managers may skim these reports to obtain personal assurance that no surprises are lurking to catch them unawares in the future. Short quarterly review meetings may be scheduled to review progress against preset goals. In Umapathy's survey, for example, 15 percent of the firms prepared budgets that were broken down on a monthly basis; 82 percent used a quarterly breakdown. Sixty-seven percent required written explanation of the causes of deviations (1987, 84, 89).

3. *Following up on significant exceptions.* If a critical performance variable is off target, managers must devote the necessary attention and resources to bring the variable back in line. The purpose of diagnostic control systems is to monitor goal achievement for critical performance variables. Little management attention is required unless a critical performance variable goes out of control.

Design Considerations

There are two accepted truisms in management control literature. First, measurement is critical to management control. Second, participants focus a disproportionate amount of attention on any variable that is measured. These observations, which have important organizational implications, have led to their own familiar set of catchphrases such as, "what you measure is what you get," "what gets measured gets managed," or "you get what you inspect, not what you expect."

To use diagnostic control systems to control any process, it must be possible to (1) develop preset standards or goals, (2) measure outputs, and (3) correct deviations from standard.[1] The first condition

---

[1] These conditions have been identified by a number of previous authors including Lawler and Rhode (1976, 42–43); Otley and Berry (1980); and Merchant (1985, 20).

implies that managers know *ex ante* what quantities and types of output are desired. Diagnostic control is difficult to implement if there is a high degree of novelty in the process to be controlled. For this reason, valid diagnostic controls are notoriously difficult to implement in an R&D laboratory. The second condition, measurability, suggests that diagnostic control is inappropriate for monitoring nebulous concepts such as "success" or "changes in business culture." While these concepts may be critical performance variables, they are difficult to measure. The final condition—ability to correct deviations—suggests that diagnostic controls are appropriate only for processes that organizational participants influence significantly.[2] Thus, earnings-per-share makes little sense as a diagnostic measure for a regional sales manager at a large international company.

We shall now consider more carefully these features of diagnostic control systems.

Goals and Motivation

Formal goals or standards, which are necessary for diagnostic control, provide focus and motivation for the achievement of critical performance targets. According to many management theorists, motivation is the central function of any management control system (Anthony 1988, 14; Lawler and Rhode 1976, 6). Clear diagnostic control systems goals, then, enhance performance (Kenis 1979).

Goal-setting provides benchmarks for identifying problems. Negative variances trigger remedial action and provide guidelines about how to analyze the causes of problems. Goal-setting also forces managers to review goals at periodic intervals, thus ensuring that opportunity-seeking behavior is in line with broader organizational objectives. Furthermore, goal-setting facilitates the coordination of action plans at various levels of the organization by forcing participants to determine if adequate resources are available to meet specific goals, and if the goals contribute to the overall strategy of the business. The diagnostic goal-setting process is a primary mechanism for

---

[2]From a systems theory perspective, a system is *controllable* if it is possible to force the system to change from one state to another state in a given time period by adjusting variables of the system (Amey 1979, 153). The ability to *influence* a system requires only that adjusting variables of the system changes the system from one state to another, not completely defined, state. Usually the performance variables of business organizations can be influenced rather than controlled.

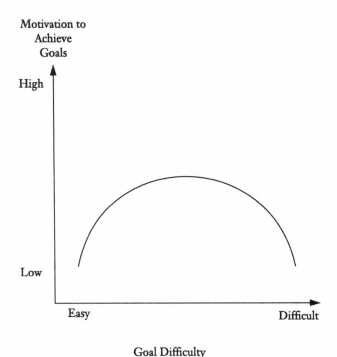

Figure 4.6   Goal Difficulty and Motivation

cascading goals from the top of the organization to the bottom and for coordinating the resources necessary to implement desired strategies.

One of the trickier issues in designing and using diagnostic controls is deciding on the level of difficulty that should exist in predetermined standards. Open-ended goals—"more is better"—are not usually desirable as research has shown that motivation is reduced when goals are not specific (Meyer, Kay, and French 1965; Tosi 1975). However, setting specific goals requires judgment about effects on motivation. A substantial body of research indicates that the desire to achieve is strongest when goals are perceived to be moderately challenging; motivation is reduced if goals are either too easy or too difficult (Stedry and Kay 1966; Hofstede 1968, 154–55; Lawler 1973, 134–35; Carroll and Tosi 1973, 41; Hopwood 1974, 61–62). If goals are too easy, people do not strive to potential. If goals are too difficult, people give up. This is reflected in the inverted U-shape curve of Figure 4.6.

Other research indicates that the perceived fairness of goals—and hence motivation—can be enhanced in certain conditions if superiors and subordinates set goals jointly. Participation by subordinates can allow more reasonable goals and the perception of reasonable goals. This relationship, however, is far from straightforward. Organizational variables such as environment, structure, and technology intervene to influence joint goal setting as do such individual variables as personality type.[3] Because of the complexity and interdependence of these relationships, our ability to make useful statements or predictions about the value of participation in goal setting remains limited.

Deciding on the level of difficulty becomes complicated because diagnostic control systems are used to achieve multiple purposes in organizations. The same diagnostic control system—a profit planning system, for example—can be used to provide motivation; to coordinate plans and resources; to provide benchmarks for corrective action; and as a basis for performance evaluation and reward. Each of these purposes may require setting performance standards at different levels of difficulty. Motivation of subordinates may require levels that reflect some degree of difficulty, or "stretch" in targets. Coordination may require a level that reflects the most probable outcome. Early warning may require setting goals at lower acceptable limits to trip alarms for important deviations. *Ex post* evaluation of either individuals or businesses may require eliminating uncontrollable factors from performance results (Barrett and Fraser 1977).

Economists and accounting theorists sometimes assume that diagnostic control systems are used solely as performance contracts between superiors and their subordinates. This assumption ignores the important role of diagnostic control systems in resource allocation, coordination, early warning, and business evaluation. Thus, mathematical models may suggest, for example, that explicit performance goals should be eliminated in favor of rewards that are a linear function of outputs, the "more is better" solution.

How do managers reconcile different levels of difficulty for different purposes? They introduce slack into the system and then adjust targets as necessary for each specific purpose. This has the side effect of ensuring that the diagnostic goals given to participants are achievable under reasonable circumstances. In a study of the incentives provided to profit center managers in twelve American companies, Merchant observed,

[3]For a review of the literature on this subject, see Brownell (1982) and Brownell and McInnes (1986).

The vast majority of profit center managers in the 12 corporations face the same budget contract: they are asked to make their budget targets and told that if they fail to do so, at least more years than not, they will face potentially severe consequences. Most of the firms place the greatest emphasis on meeting *annual* budget targets, but some also place significant emphasis on meeting *quarterly* targets and those for even shorter periods. (1989, 29–30)

While pressure to achieve diagnostic targets seems severe, Merchant also notes, "although this 'make-the-budget-or-else' contract provides potentially significant threat, the targets are set almost as minimum performance standards that effective, hardworking managers can expect to meet, even if they run into some bad luck" (p. 30).

In response to a question put to forty-four profit center managers about the probability of achieving budget targets, 89 percent reported that they believed they had at least a 75 percent chance of hitting budget targets at the time budgets were approved; 55 percent reported that they believed they had a 90 percent chance or better of hitting budget targets. *Ex post* data confirmed their assessment: 74 percent of these managers met or exceeded their budget targets in the immediately preceding year (Merchant 1989, 31–33).

Merchant speculates that managers choose highly achievable goals to improve the predictability of earnings forecasts, improve resource planning, ensure that only significant negative variances become a focus for superiors, provide a competitive compensation package, and allow organizational slack for purposes of experimentation (pp. 155–60). Argyris (1990a) further argues that superiors provide relatively easy budget goals to avoid the potential embarrassment of confronting inadequate performance.

Measurement, Comparison, and Corrective Action

Diagnostic control measurement compares outputs—either quantity or quality—to a predetermined measurement scale. Measures can be based on nominal scales (How many finished units are blue or black?), ordinal scales (Are we third or fourth in customer satisfaction rankings?), interval scales (By how much did we miss our target this month as compared to last?), and ratio scales (What is our average sales per employee?).

Diagnostic measurement focuses on errors of commission (mistakes) and shortfalls (negative variances) against goals. This focus on mistakes and negative variances represents the yin of management control. In fact, diagnostic control systems are negative feedback systems.[4] Diagnostic control reports are used primarily as confirmation that everything is "on track." Surprise is the enemy. As Anthony states, "an important control principle is that the formal performance reports should contain no surprises" (1988, 95). In other words, participants should inform managers if attention is required to get a process back on track; managers should not have to wait for formal reports. The identification of variances should trigger managerial corrective action.

Ideally, diagnostic control measures should be objective, complete, and responsive (Lawler 1976; Lawler and Rhode 1976, 42). A measure is objective when it is independently verifiable; complete when it captures all relevant actions or behaviors; and responsive when it reflects the efforts or actions of the individual being measured. These ideal attributes are seldom achieved. Figure 4.7 summarizes the major dilemmas inherent in designing measures for motivational purposes.

Objective measures provide clear guidelines about what outcomes are desired. Because objective measures are derived from known formulas, there is little ambiguity about desired results. Market share data collected by an independent survey agency, for example, leaves little ambiguity about what outcomes are desired. From a motivational perspective, then, objective measures reduce the risks of perceived unfairness.

Although diagnostic measures should be objective, they are occasionally subjective. Subjective measures rely on the personal judgments of superiors and will be effective motivators only if the superior is capable of making an accurate and informed judgment about the actions of the subordinate and only if trust between superior and subordinate is high. If the superior is not competent to make an informed judgment or if trust is low, subjective measures will not be seen as valid measures of accomplishment and may breed dissatisfaction.

Measures may also vary in their degree of completeness, the ability to capture all relevant actions or behaviors. Incomplete mea-

---

[4] Diagnostic control systems are negative feedback systems because the sign of the deviation that is derived when outputs and standards are compared is reversed in the feedback signal to adjust the process. For example, if outputs are too high (low), a signal is sent to reduce (increase) the level of inputs. More formally, if inputs are designated x, outputs y, and the process to be controlled is denoted v, the feedback signal r must correct all deviations of y from some standard. The systems output is given by $y = vx + vry = vx/(1 - vr)$ (for further discussion, see Amey [1979] p. 71).

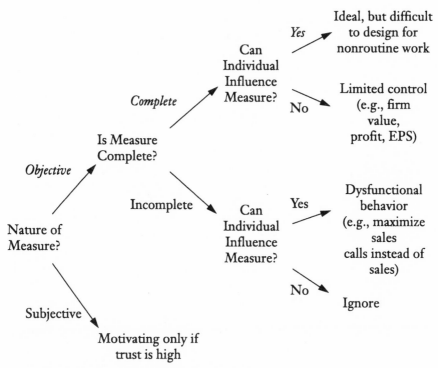

Figure 4.7   Characteristics of Diagnostic Control
Systems Measures

sures lead to dysfunctional behavior. In an attempt to build market
share through sales force productivity, for example, a regional manager might choose to measure the number of sales calls made each
week by the salesmen. But the number of sales calls per week is
an incomplete measure because it does not capture all the behaviors
necessary to sell more of the product. Using this measure, salespeople
may attempt to maximize the number of calls per day, regardless of
the potential for sales at each stop. Large customers who are difficult
to visit will be ignored in favor of small customers who are easily
accessible.

But complete measures have problems of their own. The most
complete measure is economic profit, or firm earnings. This measure
captures all the behaviors that translate into success. Unfortunately,
it includes too much. The more complete the measure, the greater
the probability that it is not responsive to individual efforts or actions.

Using this measure, marketing managers may feel, quite rightly, that doing an outstanding job will not have a noticeable effect on overall corporate earnings as their regions represent only a tiny fraction of the total business. In other words, the measure does not reflect real contribution and effort.

Accounting measures that include revenues, costs, cash flows, and profits are predominant in many diagnostic control systems because these measures are objective, reliable, and verifiable (Ijiri 1975, 36). Where quantity data are critical indicators for production or service delivery, measures tend to focus on physical units (McKinnon and Bruns 1992, chs. 1, 2). Accounting measures, however, are often inadequate indicators of actions that affect a firm's critical performance variables. When a business (for example, a pharmaceutical company) needs to invest over several accounting periods before a product can be brought to market, accounting measures make poor indicators for critical performance variables.

As a result, a number of authors have called for the rejection of accounting measures in favor of measures such as quality or customer satisfaction (Lorange and Scott Morton 1974; Eccles 1991). The success in implementing these proposals depends on the ability of managers to construct objective, complete, and responsive measures. Work by such writers as Kaplan and Norton (1992) is an attempt in this direction. Nevertheless, at the top of the organization, aggregate measures, often rooted in accounting data and profitability analyses, become more important as senior managers monitor the performance of lower level units (plants or divisions) and make trade-offs concerning resource allocation.

Objective, complete, and responsive measures—the upper path of Figure 4.7—often can be achieved for lower level jobs where task complexity, decision trade-offs, and uncontrollable events are at a minimum. Designing these measures for a plant foreman is not difficult. For higher level managerial jobs, however, finding the right balance between objectivity, completeness, and responsiveness remains a challenge. Failure to strike the right balance can result in limited control of important processes, dysfunctional behavior on the part of those being measured, and ignoring the measure altogether.

Diagnostic Control and Formal Incentives

Managers, economists, and management theorists all recognize the power of incentives in motivating behaviors. Incentives that allow people to capture the benefits of their efforts stimulate individual initiative and opportunity-seeking. Diagnostic control systems are catalysts in this process as formal incentives are linked to output measures.

Diagnostic control system incentives tend to be based on explicit formulas, which provide objectivity, define the outputs desired, and require the least amount of management attention. Objectivity provides motivation and clear direction for effort. Individuals know what they will be rewarded for and how it is to be measured. Definitions of expected outputs provide guidance as to where the attention and opportunity-seeking energy of subordinates should be focused. Finally, formulas free management attention for other tasks. Once the formula is set and agreed upon, senior managers do not need to consider how to split up and reward the marginal product of all employees. For this reason, many incentives are simply linear payouts based on a percentage of performance outputs. Usually, however, bonus incentives are tied to specific goal achievements to increase short-term motivation and ensure the achievement of important goals. Often, managers establish thresholds that withhold incentive bonuses unless minimum performance levels are achieved.

Merchant observed that diagnostic performance measures were tied to incentive compensation by formula in all twelve of the companies involved in his study of incentive systems. Moreover, eleven of the twelve firms explicitly tied incentives to *ex ante* diagnostic targets. The relevant performance standard was usually established as part of the annual budgeting process and included a variety of accounting measures such as earnings, cash flow, sales growth, and return-on-assets, as well as nonaccounting measures such as quality, shipments, delinquencies, and ratings of peer groups, and so on (Merchant 1989, 35–38, 55–58). The potentially punitive aspect of diagnostic control system incentives was noted:

> Managers who fail to achieve budget targets usually lose out on many rewards, and they may be assessed some organizational penalties. Bonuses and salary increases are obvious rewards that will be reduced if budget targets are missed. Often even more important, the managers also lose credibility, which in turn harms their promotion possibilities and their ability to sell their ideas and compete effectively for corporate resources. They are also likely to lose some autonomy, as top management is more likely to intervene in the profit centers' affairs where budget targets are being missed (Merchant 1989, 30).

Compensation incentives are used not only to reward outcomes, but also to guide opportunity-seeking in conformity with organizational strategies. As Harrison White concluded,

Compensation's conventional motivational role (giving the agent incentives to act in the principal's interest) is less important, I think, than its role in informing agents of what their responsibility is and how it changes. . . . Performance-related compensation for managers may be primarily a vehicle for defining what it is they are to do (1985, 192).

The positive motivational effects of allowing people to capture the rewards of their efforts is undeniable. However, problems in measurement coupled with the power of incentives to focus attention on dimensions being measured, make the linkage between results and rewards problematic.

We have yet to solve—and may never solve—the problem of how to measure and separate an individual's marginal contribution from the overall marginal product of the firm. When Ford launches a successful new automobile, how can senior managers calibrate the relative contribution of the design team that created the concept, the engineering team that developed and applied new technologies, the marketing team that launched the product, and the division president who oversaw the entire effort? How do we measure the contribution of a single violin player in relation to the successful season enjoyed by a symphony orchestra?

When individuals work as members of a team striving toward common organizational goals, disaggregating individual contributions is difficult. In atomistic economic markets, where autonomous self-interested individuals work at arm's length, markets can be relied upon to facilitate transactions and efficiently allocate the rewards of initiative and effort. In complex organizations, work must be bonded together by shared beliefs, group norms, and common goals; measuring the contribution of individuals who work as part of such a team is much more difficult (Williamson 1975).

Moreover, economic rewards are not the only rewards sought by participants. Noneconomic incentives, such as recognition and prestige, can be just as important. In addition to substantive economic incentives, many firms harness the power of noneconomic rewards by combining public recognition and relatively inexpensive prizes to achieve a powerful set of noneconomic formal incentives based on diagnostic control system measures. Managers at Mary Kay Cosmetics, for example, describe the role of recognition as an incentive for their sales force:

As Mary Kay herself would say, "A $5 ribbon plus $20 worth of recognition is worth more than a $25 prize." In other words, give them a check, but give it to them on stage. Then they will really respond. I would never take away the recognition element. It would be like putting my head on a chopping block. Some of the salespeople don't need the money at all, but the recognition is addictive. In fact, the top people in our sales organization motivate their units through recognition, not expensive prizes. (Simons and Weston 1990b)

Finally, the absolute level of rewards may be less important than a comparison of rewards relative to peers (Lawler 1972). The power of rewards cannot be considered independent of the effects of peer ranking that will inevitably occur by those receiving the rewards.

Dysfunctional Side-Effects

Measuring the wrong variables. The old saying, "What you measure is what you get" cuts both ways. If critical performance variables and measures are correctly specified, the organization will march unerringly toward the achievement of organizational goals. If measures and targets are incorrectly specified, the organization may march off a cliff.

In the late 1980s, Dun & Bradstreet's Credit Services Division was the subject of lawsuits and investigative reporting for overcharging clients.[5] Clients purchased subscription units that were later redeemed for services, but it was alleged that the company systematically sold more units than clients actually used. According to lawsuits, actual usage levels were either distorted or hidden from clients, who relied on sales representatives for advice on how many subscription units to purchase. Diagnostic control targets contributed to the problem. Targets focused on increasing unit sales. If the number of subscription units declined from one year to the next, rewards were reduced, thereby providing incentives to renew subscriptions at higher levels no matter what the client's actual usage. Settlements to clients and shareholders as a result of this overcharging were $38 million (Roberts 1989).

Similar stories have been reported for auto repair businesses. At Sears, for example, managers were given repair quotas and rewards for meeting them. As a result, repairs were made even if not required (Yin 1992). Sears paid $60 million to settle related lawsuits.

[5]"Dun & Bradstreet: Behind the Facade," *20/20*, ABC News, May 12, 1989.

Building slack into targets. Diagnostic control systems provide incentives for subordinates to build slack into preset goals or standards. Because diagnostic control systems draw attention to results below preset standards of performance, participants may want to create standards that are easily attainable. In so doing, the probability of negative variances is reduced, performance is less likely to be singled out for scrutiny, rewards are secure, and expectations for future performance are dampened (Argyris 1990a). If budgets are difficult to achieve, participants may manipulate standards by building in a cushion of performance slack.

Sometimes adding slack may even jeopardize organizational survival. When managers at General Motors were required to monitor quality defects on a scale of 100, they were dismayed to learn that cars coming off the assembly line had in excess of 40 defects on average, yielding a score below 60. Rather than attend to the cause of the problems, managers changed the measurement scale to score defects against an absolute scale of 145 points; thus, the average car with 45 defects was now awarded a point score of 100. Factories that produced cars with only 15 quality defects were awarded prizes, and quality continued to decline, ultimately threatening General Motors' ability to compete against higher quality rivals (Keller 1989, 29–30).

Gaming the system. Diagnostic control systems may tempt individuals to "game" the system to enhance rewards. Managers of a credit card company that followed a high-volume, low-cost strategy wanted to encourage efficiency in their customer service operation. Employees were measured and rewarded for maximizing the "number of calls answered per day" and minimizing "talk time per call." When a cardholder asked a difficult question that would take time to answer or required looking up additional information, some employees merely transferred the call to another department. Talk time was minimized in line with desired goals, but the cardholder on the other end of the line was left frustrated and angry.[6]

Under IBM's old strategy, managers in the marketing and services division were measured and rewarded on their ability to meet product quotas. Branch managers received credits toward their quotas for equipment sold to businesses through independent retailers in their area. A marketing representative was entitled to credit for such

---

[6]From a paper prepared by N. M. Gandy for the Harvard M.B.A. course Strategic Management Systems, 1992.

sales even if he or she had not been involved. As a result, some representatives and managers spent time driving around their territories searching for free credits instead of generating new business (Simons and Weston 1990a).

Other techniques. The types of distortion encountered with diagnostic control system targets and data are limited only by human ingenuity.[7] In addition to gaming—engaging in behaviors to influence the measure that do not further organizational goals—techniques include:

- Smoothing—altering the timing and flow of data without changing the underlying transactions being measured (e.g., adjusting accounting accruals);
- Biasing—transmitting only data that are perceived to be favorable (e.g., reporting only targets that have been achieved); and
- Illegal acts—violation of organizational rules and/or laws (Birnberg, Turopolec, and Young, 1983).

In his study of the budgeting practices of more than 400 U.S. firms, Umapathy found budget games and manipulation were widespread:

Deferring a needed expenditure [was the budget game] used with the highest frequency. . . . Getting approvals after money was spent, shifting funds between accounts to avoid budget overruns, and employment of contract labor to avoid exceeding headcount limits are the other relatively popular games. Almost all respondents state that they engage in one or more of the budget games. . . . Managers either did not accept the budgetary targets and opted to beat the system, or they felt pressured to achieve the budgetary targets at any cost. (1987, 90)

Brown's return-on-investment measure was designed originally as a tool for resource allocation. When it was later used to evaluate the performance of individual managers, manipulative behaviors to maximize ROI, such as under-investment in assets to minimize the denominator of the ratio and altering accounting conventions to maximize the numerator, became well known (Dearden 1969).

The use of diagnostic control systems to measure an individual's performance and calibrate rewards can lead to innovation. Some-

---

[7] See, for example, Ridgway (1956); Merchant (1985, ch. 7); Argyris (1990a); Merchant (1990); Bruns and Merchant (1990).

times, however, the opportunistic actions are not those contemplated when the measures and incentive formulas were designed, and they may, in fact, be harmful to the interests of the firm. The nuclear accident at Chernobyl had its antecedents in distortion of control system information:

Operators and local engineers concealed small mishaps from their superiors. Often they were not even recorded in the operational log books. More serious accidents and shutdowns were covered up by nuclear plant administrators, because their bonuses and rewards depended on good records. Construction and design faults were covered up by the ministerial and atomic energy bureaucracies, which had vested interests in the good image of the nuclear industry. (Holloway 1990, 5)

As one manager who works in one of General Electric's highly competitive businesses stated, "Pressure builds to deliver. Give someone a budget and it will be met 98% of the time. There is a natural tendency to do what has to be done to meet budget. This is generally healthy. But, if you don't tell them to stay clean, they will assume by omission that it's OK to bend the rules. We must always send a double message: we need more, but do it honestly" (Simons 1989).

Internal Controls

Diagnostic control systems operate effectively only if reported data are accurate and complete. Management-by-exception cannot work if exceptions are masked by inaccurate data collection and reporting procedures. Internal controls, designed to safeguard assets from misappropriation and ensure reliable accounting records and information systems, are critical to ensure the integrity of diagnostic control systems. Internal controls are the detailed, procedural checks and balances that include the following:

Structural Safeguards
> Active Audit Committee of the Board
> Independent Internal Audit Function
> Segregation of Duties
> Defined levels of authorization
> Restricted access to valuable assets

Staff Safeguards
> Adequate expertise and training for all accounting, control, and
> internal audit staff

Sufficient resources
Rotation in key jobs
System Safeguards
Complete and accurate recordkeeping
Adequate documentation and audit trail
Relevant and timely management reporting
Restricted access to information systems and data bases

Internal controls are different from boundary systems, which specify risks to be avoided. Internal controls specify the detailed procedures and safeguards for information handling, transaction processing, and recordkeeping. Staff groups typically install and maintain internal controls, which are then evaluated periodically by internal and external auditors. Internal controls are essential to ensure the integrity of the other systems that managers use to implement strategy (Figure 4.8). All too often, the right hand column of the front page on the *Wall Street Journal* features some hapless manager as the casualty of a business failure that resulted from inadequate internal controls.

The Role for Staff Groups

Diagnostic control systems can conserve management attention only because of the amount of attention that staff groups devote to these systems. Staff groups receive authority from senior managers to maintain and operate diagnostic control systems. Accountants, sales planners, engineers, and quality control experts are the critical functionaries and gatekeepers of diagnostic control systems. Not only do these staff groups maintain and operate diagnostic control systems, they also monitor the accuracy of the data supplied by business managers. When diagnostic control systems are important in monitoring the health of a business and managers of the business are supplying data to the system, centralized staff groups should audit the integrity of the system and its information.

The heavy reliance on staff groups in the diagnostic control process yields four organizational benefits:

1. Attention: staff groups lift the monitoring burden from the shoulders of business managers and thereby free scarce managerial attention.
2. Efficiency: efficiencies in the diagnostic control process can be

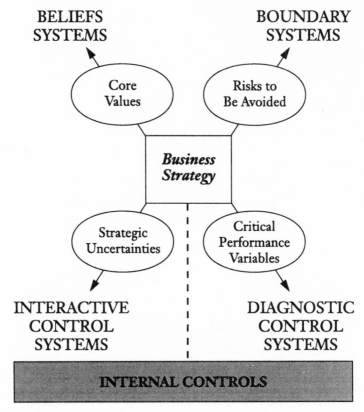

Figure 4.8 Internal Controls: The Foundation for
Effective Control

achieved through staff specialization. This is often manifested
by a centralization of staff functions at head office locations.
3. Effectiveness: utilizing professionally trained experts ensures
that the latest information and control technologies are applied
to gain the most impact from the diagnostic control processes.
(See Appendix B for a discussion of gains from information technology.)
4. Integrity: independent staff professionals can supply the necessary safeguards and oversight to ensure the integrity of data.

The power delegated to control specialists can, however, lead to
organizational resentment because staff groups highlight and expose
negative variances for corrective action. In this way, staff experts
show senior managers that they are adding value to the organization,

but there is always the risk that staff groups will become overzealous in searching for errors and shortfalls. As part of their responsibilities, staff specialists may tend to overemphasize management errors and failures.

If left unchecked, the tendency to search for negative variances can create the perception that managers have to fail for staff groups to add value. Argyris noted this tendency forty years ago in a study of budget supervisors and factory supervisors:

The budget people, therefore, see their task as one of always examining, always analyzing, always looking for new ways to make the plant more efficient. Such a task is primarily a critical one. Its primary emphasis seems to be, "never be completely satisfied." One budget staff man described this as follows:

> Ours is a tough job. The function of budgets is to be critical. Budget people should never be satisfied. They should always try to find new and better ways of doing things.

There is, therefore, an important emphasis made on budget people *constantly finding things that are "sour,"* looking for weaknesses and, in general, looking for things that are *wrong*, not right. (1952, 6)

After forty years of additional research and study, Argyris confirmed his original assessment,

[According to the authors of management accounting textbooks], budgets change human behavior, compel managers to look ahead, force executives to think, remove unconscious bias, and search out weakness. Strictly speaking budgets do not do these things. It is individuals who implement these actions. If the authors mean that accountants should use budgets to compel, force, etc. line management then they are recommending a strategy of implementation that will probably backfire. Such unilateral and coercive activity will activate individual and organizational defensive routines that are over-protective and anti-learning. (1990a, 509)

If diagnostic control systems are to function effectively, managers must be aware of these tendencies and work to counteract them.

Asset Acquisition Systems as Diagnostic Control Systems

Chapter 3 examined how asset acquisition systems (capital budgeting systems) can create boundaries to constrain current strate-

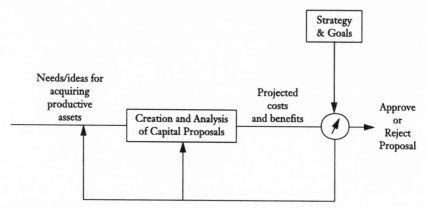

Figure 4.9 Asset Acquisition Systems as Diagnostic
Control Systems

gic options. Asset acquisition systems also play an important diagnostic role in monitoring acquisition proposals to ensure fit with intended strategies. As illustrated in Figure 4.9, opportunities for acquiring productive assets are documented in formal asset acquisition proposals. Estimated performance measures are developed for such variables as net present value, cash flow, payback, and ROI. Before proceeding with investment, these measures are tested against the preset economic standards and goals stipulated in planning documents. Based on this comparison, the proposal, and the underlying substance of the transaction, may be adjusted to improve the likely outcome of committing resources.

Many have suggested adding a second diagnostic stage, commonly termed a "post-audit," to improve the diagnostic capabilities of asset acquisition systems. This idea is captured in Figure 4.10. If the first stage of the process yields a green light to go ahead with the acquisition, the "post-audit" stage measures the realized costs and benefits of the acquisition against the projections that were calculated during the screening stage. Post-auditing, of course, cannot be completed until the asset is productive, and the realized economic and strategic benefits cannot be calculated until the stream of costs and benefits becomes predictable.

However, it is difficult to use post-auditing as a diagnostic tool for significant, long-lived assets for three reasons. First, projected costs and benefits developed in the original proposal become invalid as the time frame lengthens. Assumptions that led to original cost/

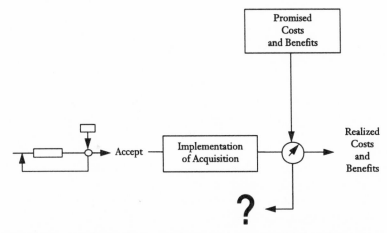

Figure 4.10   Adding Post-Audit to Asset Acquisition Systems

benefit projections become inaccurate over time. This inaccuracy makes variance data increasingly less useful for any investment that spans several years or decades.

Second, to the extent that accurate variance data can be developed, it is not clear what can or should be done with this information. The commitment to invest will have been made long ago, based on the necessarily uncertain information available at that time. Attempting to evaluate decisions with full *ex post* knowledge of all unforeseeable events is a trap that utility regulators sometimes fall into. During the benign 1980s, for example, regulators criticized utility executives for having created excess capacity by building large generating facilities in the previous decade. Regulators forgot the energy crisis and demand projections that had made construction a good bet in the 1970s.

Moreover, from the perspective of managers working in dynamic and uncertain markets, there is neither an opportunity to adjust the decision itself nor an opportunity to learn how to predict more accurately in the future. Because of these caveats, managers cannot tie rewards and incentives to diagnostic asset acquisition measurements. And, without using formal incentives, a diagnostic model is not likely to capture the attention of managers.

Summary

Business and government organizations cannot function without diagnostic control systems. Many of today's financial measures (ROI, capital budgeting procedures, internal profit targets) were invented and popularized in the early 1900s by the Dupont Company and linked together in the 1920s by General Motors. Today, diagnostic control systems are ubiquitous. These systems assist in the monitoring and accomplishment of critical performance variable goals, financial and nonfinancial, by ensuring an explicit top-down linkage of intended strategies to lower-level goals and the coordination of resources and action plans; by providing motivation to achieve organizational goals; by serving as a basis for evaluation of businesses and managers; and by providing benchmarks for corrective action. Because diagnostic control systems are tools of strategy implementation, designing these systems requires a careful analysis and understanding of critical performance variables.

To assure expected results and minimize dysfunctional effects, measures should be objective, complete, and responsive, but these ideal attributes are difficult to achieve for managerial tasks. Measurement and goal setting are the key design parameters of diagnostic control systems, and each presents its own set of design problems. These problems are magnified because diagnostic control systems have the potential to focus opportunity seeking in inappropriate ways and because the power of these systems is magnified by linking achievement with extrinsic rewards.

Staff professionals are the gatekeepers for diagnostic control systems. Senior managers involve themselves in diagnostic control systems only periodically. Above all, diagnostic control systems provide assurance that the machinery of the organization is functioning and that intended goals and strategies are achieved without constant monitoring and oversight. Through management-by-exception, these systems play a critical role in maximizing ROM.

CHAPTER 5

Interactive Control Systems:
Adapting to Competitive Environments

Managing the tension between creative innovation and predictable goal achievement is the essence of management control. Effective managers scan for disruptive changes that signal the need to reconfigure organization structures, capabilities, and product technologies. Some have argued that management control systems act as filters that homogenize information, thereby removing signals of disruptive environmental change (Hedberg and Jönsson 1978). According to this view, management control systems limit search routines and experimentation—hardly a prescription for innovation and opportunity-seeking.

While diagnostic control systems do constrain innovation and opportunity-seeking to ensure the predictable goal achievement needed for intended strategies, other management control systems produce exactly the opposite effects. These control systems stimulate search and learning, allowing new strategies to emerge as participants throughout the organization respond to perceived opportunities and threats.

Studies in a variety of management disciplines have arrived at a similar conclusion: competitive pressure is a catalyst for innovation and adaptation. Porter studied the major industries of ten nations to find that national industries subject to intense domestic competitive pressures innovate and adapt more rapidly than industries that are protected from market pressures (1990, 86). Chandler studied administrative innovation in large firms in the early part of the century and concluded that competitive pressures caused these firms to adapt their internal structures creatively to be more responsive to changing markets (1962, 303–309). As the CEO of a highly innovative and successful corporation stated, "You won't get innovation without pressure" (Taylor 1990, 98).

Management control systems play a critical role in creating competitive pressures within the organization to innovate and adapt. Successful adaptation in competitive markets requires organizations to break out of limited search routines (Cyert and March 1963, 123–25). New ideas and experiments must be encouraged at all levels. For control systems to facilitate this process, they must have special design attributes.

In Chapter 4, I drew an analogy between diagnostic control systems and a home heating thermostat: set the temperature and the system self-regulates. This type of automatic feedback system is not useful in the face of major changes in competitive dynamics. In order not to be blind-sided in rapidly changing markets, the search for relevant information must not be limited by diagnostic routines and procedures. Instead, senior managers need a measurement system more like the one used by the national weather service. Ground stations all over the country monitor temperature, barometric pressure, relative humidity, cloud cover, wind direction and velocity, and precipitation. Balloons and satellites provide additional data. These data are monitored continuously and fed to a central location where they can be used to search for patterns of change. Based on these intelligence data, forecasts of impending conditions can be made or revised in light of changing circumstances.

To activate a similar process in business organizations, senior managers must encourage continuous search activity and create information networks inside the organization to scan and report critical changes. Individuals must share information with others:

There are limits to the volume of information you can use intelligently. You can keep up with only so many books, articles, memos, and news services. Given a limit to the volume of information that anyone can process, the network becomes an important screening device. It is an army of people processing information who can call your attention to key bits—keeping you up to date on developing opportunities, warning you of impending disasters. This second-hand information is often fuzzy or inaccurate, but it serves to signal something to be looked into more carefully. (Burt 1992, 62)

How can top managers motivate organizational participants to launch intelligence balloons, continually measure environmental vari-

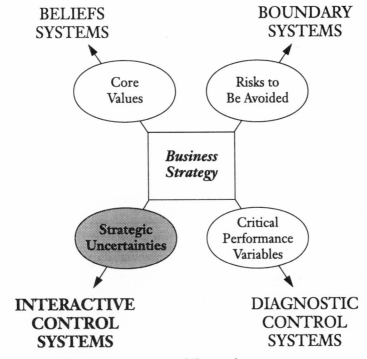

Figure 5.1   The Fourth Lever of Control

ables, and share the information with others for comparison and sense-making? Given large opportunity space and differing experiences of people in the organization, how do senior managers communicate where to look for discontinuous change? With limited attention, how do top managers ensure that sufficient information processing capacity is reserved for communication of these potentially important signals? In this chapter, we examine how senior managers use interactive control systems to build internal pressure to break out of narrow search routines, stimulate opportunity-seeking, and encourage the emergence of new strategic initiatives. As the fourth lever of control, these systems focus attention on strategic uncertainties and enable strategic renewal (Figure 5.1).

Strategic Uncertainties

If a business is to seize emerging opportunities—to innovate and adapt—managers must ask themselves more than "What are the critical things that this business must do well to achieve its intended strategy?" They must also ask themselves, "What assumptions or external shocks could block the achievement of our vision for the future?"

Strategic uncertainties are the uncertainties and contingencies that could threaten or invalidate the current strategy of the business. Uncertainty, in general, derives from a difference in the information required to perform a task and the amount of information possessed by the organization (Galbraith 1977, 36). Strategic uncertainties derive from senior management's perception of the known and unknown contingencies that could threaten or invalidate the assumptions underlying the current strategy.

Pepsi is typical of consumer goods companies that compete by selling mature products and brands. Managers in these firms are expert at exploiting strong brand franchises and extending product life cycles for seemingly indefinite periods. Strategic uncertainties for these businesses relate to changes in customer tastes that could undermine the attractiveness of their products. For Pepsi, uncertainties include consumer response to the pricing, promotion, and packaging moves by Coke; changes in preferences for sweet carbonated drinks; propensity to substitute fruit-based drinks; perceived health risks of artificial sweeteners; and so forth. Significant changes in these consumer sentiments can erode the value of the brand. Market share indicators are real-time gauges of customer buying habits that may signal trends to be watched. As the manager of a consumer goods company stated, "Every week, month, and quarter, I review each brand's sales in units and dollars. I look for downward trends and, equally important, for signs of unusual vitality. If a brand starts doing something, I get interested. What have we done that's new? Have we changed the packaging to say something new to the consumer?" (Simons 1991, 55). Strategic uncertainties are in a constant state of flux and, therefore, cannot be programmed and monitored on management-by-exception basis.

Like critical performance variables, strategic uncertainties are uniquely determined for each business based on its current business strategy and the strategic vision of its senior managers. The product/market strategy recorded in planning documents and goals usually covers one to three years, but a vision of how the business will evolve over a five- to ten-year time frame is an integral part of business strategy.

Consider, for example, a business in the hospital supply industry that competes as the low-cost producer of intravenous drug delivery products. This business manufactures and sells large quantities of standardized, disposable products such as syringes, wipes, tubing, and plasma containers. Critical performance variables for this low-cost, high-volume strategy relate to product quality and manufacturing and distribution efficiencies. These critical performance variables are monitored carefully by diagnostic control systems. Managers meet weekly for twenty minutes to review a single sheet of paper that highlights performance statistics for a dozen critical variables. These performance factors are so well understood that the meeting typically focuses on a quick review of the actions that have already been taken to keep everything within expected performance tolerances.

These factors are not strategic uncertainties perceived by senior managers. Instead, the strategic uncertainties they perceive relate to fundamental changes in drug delivery technology, which could undermine the ability of the business to deliver products valued by the market. What if advances in technology lead to ways of delivering drugs orally, or through skin patches, or through some other, as yet uncontemplated, technology? What if the nature of drug technology changes? Could the business adapt? Will it be a leader or a follower? These are the questions that keep senior managers awake at night.

Exhibit 5.1 summarizes the distinctions between strategic uncertainties and critical performance variables.

Interactive Control Systems

Interactive control systems are formal information systems managers use to involve themselves regularly and personally in the decision activities of subordinates. Based on the unique strategic un-

	Critical Performance Variables	Strategic Uncertainties
Recurring question	What must we do well to achieve our intended strategy?	What assumptions or shocks could derail the achievement of our vision for the future?
Focus on	Implementation of intended strategy	Formation of emerging strategy
Driven by	Staff analysis	Top management perception
Search for	The correct answer	The correct question

Exhibit 5.1 Distinctions Between Critical Performance Variables and Strategic Uncertainties

certainties they perceive, managers use these systems to activate search. Some managers term these systems their "personal hot buttons." Interactive control systems focus attention and force dialogue throughout the organization. They provide frameworks, or agendas, for debate, and motivate information gathering outside of routine channels.

John Sculley describes the use of such a system during his tenure at Pepsi:

> Pepsi's top managers would carry in their wallets little charts with the latest key Nielsen figures. They became such an important part of my life that I could quote them on any product in any market. We would pore over the data, using it to search for Coke's vulnerable points where an assault could successfully be launched, or to explore why Pepsi slipped a fraction of a percentage point in the game. . . . The Nielsens defined the ground rules of competition for everyone at Pepsi. They were at the epicenter of all we did. They were the non-public body count of the Cola Wars. . . . The company wasn't always this way. The man at the front of the table made it so. (1987, 2, 6–7)

An interactive system is *not* a unique type of control system: many types of control systems can be used interactively by senior managers. In the hospital supply company described earlier, managers use interactive control systems to focus on new technologies and how they might be applied to their business. Meeting for day-long sessions once a month, senior managers and subordinates throughout the organization pore over analyses that provide insight into the product introductions of competitors, emerging technology in adjacent industries, and how technology integration issues affect their product lines. Senior managers make the control system interactive by their continual personal involvement in establishing new programs and milestones, monthly reviews of progress and action plans, and regular follow-up of new market intelligence. Information from these meetings triggers new projects and long-term reviews of current product lines. As one of these managers stated, "One of my key jobs is to identify which should be the key programs—to emphasize these and de-emphasize everything else. I really work those programs and everyone understands that. People get frustrated with me because I am the world's worst planner, but they don't realize that the real plans are laid into those programs" (Simons 1991, 54).

All interactive control systems have four defining characteristics:

1. Information generated by the system is an important and recurring agenda addressed by the highest levels of management.
2. The interactive control system demands frequent and regular attention from operating managers at all levels of the organization.
3. Data generated by the system are interpreted and discussed in face-to-face meetings of superiors, subordinates, and peers.
4. The system is a catalyst for the continual challenge and debate of underlying data, assumptions, and action plans.[1]

The specific control system a senior manager chooses to use interactively focuses the attention of the entire organization on the area where the senior manager is focusing his or her personal attention. Sculley describes how the interactive control system in use at Pepsi affected managerial behavior:

No matter where I was at any time of the day, when the Nielsen flash came out, I wanted to be the first to know about it. I didn't mind a problem, but I hated surprises. The last thing I'd want was Kendall [Pepsi's CEO] calling for an explanation behind a weak number without having had the chance to see it myself. I'd scribble the details down on the back of an envelope or whatever else was convenient. Within an hour, some sixty or seventy people at Pepsi also would get the results and begin to work on them. (1987, 6)

As Lawler and Rhode note, organization participants are selective in what they attend to: "What is noticed is a joint function of the distinctiveness of the stimuli and a member's learning which messages have important personal consequences for him or her and which do not" (1976, 26–27). With the same data in everyone's hands, subordinates learn quickly that the information generated by the interactive control system has important personal consequences. In face-to-face meetings, senior managers challenge subordinates to explain any unforeseen changes in their business or suggested action plans and the assumptions that underlie their analyses. In preparation for these meetings, participants learn to call on their own peers and subordinates to help interpret the changing patterns revealed in the data. In

---

[1]It is important to understand that the unit of analysis for these ideas is the "system," not the degree of interaction among organizational participants. At lower organizational levels, similar interactive processes may also occur, but these interactions are not the focus of this analysis. An "interactive control system" is limited, by definition, to a system that is an important and recurring agenda addressed by the highest levels of management.

this way, participants build their own information systems that inform them of changing patterns and allow them to respond with new action plans. In one large company, for example, the senior manager used a highly interactive goal-setting system. This executive carried a brown leather binder with tabs for relevant project groupings. He used the information in the binder to manage the agendas of the regular meetings he held to discuss changing market conditions and review proposed action plans relating to the timing of new product roll-outs, advertising campaigns, and pricing decisions. The binder was so important to him that when he was photographed for the firm's annual report, the binder rested prominently under his hands. To be able to respond to his questions and challenges, subordinate managers created their own "brown binders" and carried them with them as they went about their day-to-day tasks.

Interactive control systems are used to guide the bottom-up emergence of strategy. In the emergent model, individuals throughout the organization act on their own initiative to seize unexpected opportunities and deal with problems. Some of these actions will be tactically important; others will not. Successful experiments will be repeated and expanded. Over time, the organization will adjust its strategies to capitalize on the learning that resulted from testing these new ideas. Sculley, for example, explains how a local experiment eventually became a new strategy for Pepsi.

We fought hard for a meager 7 percent share against Coke's 37 percent. It was hardly a contest. Out of sheer desperation, Larry Smith . . . urged an advertising effort more powerful than Pepsi's lifestyle approach. Not wanting to tamper with our hugely successful Pepsi Generation campaign, Pepsi advertising executives and [our advertising agency] resisted. Undaunted, Smith hired his own advertising agency in Texas and dispatched his vice president of marketing to help it put together something that would represent a radical departure from what we or any other company had ever done before. The result amounted to one of the most devastating advertising and promotional campaigns ever devised. The Texas agency called it the "Pepsi Challenge." (1987, 43–44)

As this local experiment, unsanctioned by senior management, was tested and rolled out to new markets, a new strategy emerged:

We treated each Challenge as a major event, a battle to be fought in our long-term war against Coke. Weeks before a Challenge would debut, we would begin quality tests on the product. If it failed to measure up, we

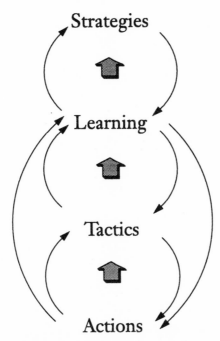

Figure 5.2 The Emergent Strategy Process

would improve its taste so that a subgoal of the contest was to upgrade the overall quality of our product. (p. 49)

Figure 5.2 illustrates how local actions can build momentum and, through learning, coalesce into new strategies. Experimentation and testing of ideas—an action orientation—can lead to strategies that were not originally contemplated by senior managers. For example, during interactive reviews of operations, senior managers of an international bank learned that some branch managers had created surprisingly profitable sidelines by offering special services and products to wealthy individuals and their businesses. A study, which was commissioned to learn the extent of this sideline, revealed just how widespread and profitable this type of business had become. In time, senior managers realized the potential of this specialty business, and the bank abandoned its old strategy of providing a full complement of international services in favor of a niche strategy that focused primarily on wealthy customers and their businesses.

Although Figure 5.2 suggests a serendipitous process of learning through experimentation, the process need not be random and uncon-

trolled. By focusing attention on strategic uncertainties, interactive
control systems can guide and shape this emergent, bottom-up
process.

Senior management's use of an interactive control system as a
catalyst for new strategies can be found in any industry or business.
While Sculley used the Nielsen ratings as a catalyst for innovation,
at USA Today, senior managers use the information contained in a
simple package of reports delivered each Friday:

Every Friday afternoon, I get a package of three management reports that I
study religiously. Together, these three reports give me a picture of how
we've done in the week just completed and what condition we are in for the
upcoming few weeks. The data in the Friday Packet range from year-to-date
figures to daily and account-specific information. So, I get a look at the big
picture as well as enough detail to identify specific vulnerabilities and the
source of any problems. . . . I keep it in my bottom drawer. It's always at
my fingertips. It's very important that we look at it line by line. I look for
dramatic increases and dramatic decreases. These reports surface problems
and opportunities very quickly. (Simons and Weston 1990e, 4)

Senior management's strategic vision at USA Today is to compete in the general-interest news market by offering advertisers an
integrated marketing tool that combines national coverage with regional customization. Strategic uncertainties revolve around changes
that might affect advertiser interest in marketing tools such as USA
Today, specifically changes in the strategy of client businesses and
changes in the health or structure of major industries. Senior managers schedule face-to-face meetings each week with key participants to
analyze and interpret data contained in the Friday reports: advertising
volume against plan, committed future volume by issue, and new
business by class of client. From these meetings, significant innovations have been proposed to deal with unexpected downturns and
to capitalize on unanticipated opportunities. Innovations—some of
which led to new market strategies—included the launching of a new
market survey service for automotive clients; introduction of frac-
tional color advertising; selling exclusive free standing inserts; and the
use of circulation salespeople to sell ad space in regional locations.

Turner Construction Company, the nation's largest construction
firm, also uses an interactive control system. The company's strategy
is to build long-term relationships that generate repeat business with
active owners and their architects. The key to success is customizing
a relationship to meet the needs of each owner. Turner is not a low-

cost competitor. Instead, it uses its reputation for quality and effective management to secure business. Strategic uncertainties include changes in owner psychology, loss of reputation in the trade, balance of risk and conservatism in the financial management of projects, and the mix and quality of staff. The interactive project management system brings the entire project team together for face-to-face reviews every six weeks. New ideas are generated and strategies for individual clients are revised as a result of these meetings. A vice-president commented,

Some people may think that we spend too much time dealing with the contingencies in the project management system, but I don't think that is true. The time we spend here is really forcing our managers to keep revising their strategy with our clients on each job. We keep asking ourselves, "Are we doing the proper evaluation, providing the best product, and the best quality?" (Simons and Weston 1990d, 12)

Other businesses use different kinds of interactive control systems. A leveraged buyout firm uses a Deal Activity reporting system interactively. Principals and deal-makers meet weekly to pore over data categorized under such headings as "long-shot," "possibility," and "in-process" to challenge and debate assumptions and action plans. New strategies emerge from these heated discussions.[2]

Harold Geneen, the legendary CEO of ITT, describes the exhilaration of participating in meetings to discuss performance data and expectations related to strategic uncertainties:

Not only did we learn and get help from one another, not only did we achieve speed and directness in handling our problems, but our meetings often were charged with such dynamism and enthusiasm that at times we worked with a feeling of sheer exhilaration. Generating new ideas that were not on anyone's agenda, we came up with new products, new ventures, new ways of doing things. (1984, 106)

Performance pressure stimulates innovation and new strategic initiatives. Learning occurs throughout the organization as attention is focused on information contained in the interactive control system.

Figure 5.3 illustrates how interactive control systems translate senior management vision into new strategies. In the upper left-hand quadrant of the figure is *business strategy*, the agreed-upon competitive plan. Guiding the current business plan is senior management's strate-

---

[2] From a paper prepared by Robert Rosenfeld for the Harvard M.B.A. course Strategic Management Systems, 1989.

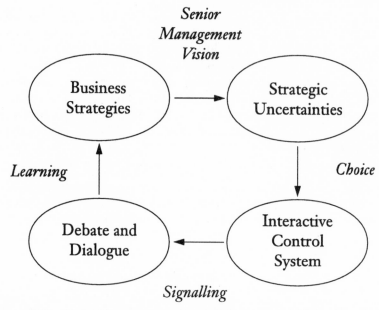

Figure 5.3   Using Interactive Control Systems to Translate Senior Management Vision into New Strategies

gic vision for the future of that business. Because of the uncertainties and dynamics of competitive markets, most managers will admit they do not fully comprehend the detailed changes necessary to move from today's competitive position to the desired competitive position of the future.

By choosing to use a control system interactively, top managers signal their preferences for search, ratify important decisions, and maintain and activate surveillance throughout the organization. All subordinate managers will engage in the interactive dialogue to the extent demanded by their position. Thus, the system may remain interactive down three or four levels in the organization, until subordinates are too junior to be directly involved with the system (Figure 5.4).

Through the dialogue, debate, and learning that surrounds the interactive process, new strategies emerge. Attention to the interactive control system emanates from the energy and personal interest of senior managers who use the interactive control system to leverage ROM. All other control systems will be used diagnostically. Thus, if the organization has *n* control systems—planning systems, cost accounting systems, human resource systems, brand revenue sys-

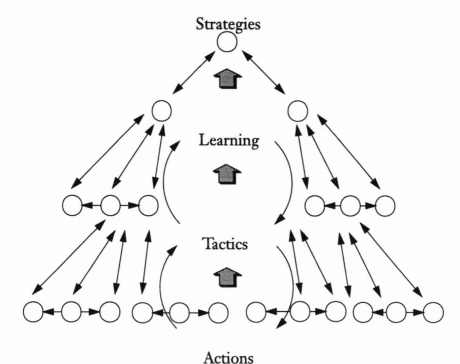

Strategies

Learning

Tactics

Actions

Figure 5.4 Interactive Control Stimulates Information Sharing and New Strategies

tems, project monitoring systems, capital-acquisition systems, profit planning systems, and so forth—one of those systems will be used interactively and $(n - 1)$ systems will be used diagnostically.

Linking the Concept of Interactive Control Systems to Other Theory

The phenomenon of senior managers using identical control systems in different ways based on attention patterns has not been documented previously in management control literature, but there are parallels in other disciplines.

In Psychology

In psychology, Ellen Langer draws a distinction between what she terms "mindlessness" and "mindfulness." Mindlessness refers to individual behaviors that are automatic and unthinking. They are learned

through habit, rules, and accepted classification categories. Driving a
car on the right side of the road, dressing appropriately for work,
and following the same route every day are examples of this automatic
unthinking behavior. Mindfulness, in contrast, is concerned with the
creation of new categories, openness to new information, and awareness of multiple perspectives (Langer 1989, 62). Langer argues that a
preoccupation with *outcomes* can make us mindless, whereas mindfulness is an orientation to the *processes* that lead to outcomes (p. 75).
Recall that diagnostic control monitors outcomes, while interactive
control focuses on process.

In line with the theme of attention allocation that underlies this
theory of control, Langer argues,

To understand why it is not necessary to be mindful about everything all
of the time, think of the brain as a large corporation, with a Chief Executive
Officer. This CEO is charged with monitoring the overall functioning of
the corporation and its transactions with the outside world—but does not,
cannot, and should not actively monitor everything. The job of maintaining
the heating system at corporate headquarters, for example, is routinely delegated to the custodial staff. The CEO need not attend to it unless and until
it requires a major investment for replacement. Similarly most of us can
routinely delegate the responsibility for our breathing. We need not become
"mindful" of it until a cold, a passionate kiss, or preparation for a marathon
makes breathing a problem. Many complex activities, such as driving a car,
require keen attention in the early learning stages but don't require mindfulness later on. The effective person—like the effective CEO—allocates
attention wisely, choosing where and when to be mindful.

A mindful CEO can be mindful on two levels: by simply resolving the
crisis in a mindful manner, or by using it as an opportunity for innovation. . . . This second-order mindfulness, choosing what to be mindful
about, is something that we can be doing all the time. Though we cannot
and would not want to be mindful of everything simultaneously, we can
always be mindful of something. The most important function task for any
CEO, and for the rest of us, is choosing what to be mindful about. Rather
than spending all day inspecting every expense account or widget in the
factory, the mindfully mindful executive chooses where to pay attention.
(pp. 198–99)

In Leadership Theory

This view is expanded by Richard Cyert, an organization scholar and
former president of Carnegie-Mellon University. Cyert argues that

a leader not only chooses where to allocate his or her attention but also signals where other participants should allocate their attention.

My definition of leadership is that the leader controls the allocation of the attention focus of the participants in the organization. . . . In any organization where managers dominate, structured rules tend to influence the allocation of attention, but the leader will try to capture the attention focus of the participants so that their attention is allocated to the areas that the leader considers important. . . .

The issues or problems on which the leader attempts to focus attention reflect, at least in part, the vision of the organization that exists in the leader's mind. . . . This vision will change over time as the leader gets feedback from the organization's performance. As the vision changes, so does the priority of individual issues and problems to which the leader wishes to allocate the attention of participants. Organizations are dynamic, and attention allocation is an ongoing and always necessary process. (1990, 32)

In Organization and Systems Theory

In concert with the idea that interactive control systems guide the allocation of attention and the gathering of information about strategic uncertainties, Cyert and March argue that search behavior will be directed to areas in which the organization is vulnerable. Those areas are defined as the activities for which connections with major goals are difficult to calculate concretely (Cyert and March 1963, 122). In these areas, learning needs are high. Decisions are nonroutine, unstructured, and affect substantial portions of the organization. Increased uncertainty requires organizations to process more information (Galbraith 1977, 37). Increased investment in formal information and control systems provides channels to move additional information up and down the organizational hierarchy.

Ackoff (1971) notes that most systems are capable of learning but differentiates between homeostatic feedback systems, which seek to maintain their state in changing environments by internal adjustment, such as a heating thermostat, and adaptive systems, which have structures that change to adapt to changing environments. He argues that some systems reduce variety and others increase variety. This distinction is analogous to the distinction made here between diagnostic control systems, which reduce variety, and interactive control systems, which increase variety. Senior managers use interactive control systems to stimulate organizational learning and the emergence of new strategies.[3]

After realizing that a new strategic initiative requires solutions and capabilities that the organization does not possess, Argyris and Schön describe the learning that becomes necessary:

Managers . . . undertake an inquiry which resolves the conflicting requirements. The results of their inquiry will take the form of a restructuring of organizational norms, and very likely a restructuring of strategies and assumptions associated with those norms, which must then be embedded in the images and maps which encode organizational theory-in-use.

We call this sort of learning *double-loop*. There is in this sort of episode a double feedback loop which connects the detection of error not only to strategies and assumptions for effective performance but to the very norms which define effective performance. (1978, 22)

Diagnostic control systems facilitate single loop learning; interactive control systems facilitate double loop learning. The single loop learning keeps a process within desired bounds; double loop learning leads to question about the very basis upon which strategies have been constructed.

In Strategic Management

Robert Burgelman's work (1983c, 1991) on the nature and context of the strategy process is also useful in grounding the concept of interactive control systems. Consistent with the distinction between a top-down strategy process and a bottom-up emergent strategy process, Burgelman distinguishes between "induced" and "autonomous" strategic behavior. Induced strategic behavior focuses on fitting an organization's distinctive competencies to the environment through administrative mechanisms, such as planning, organizational goals, and reference to critical performance variables. These administrative mechanisms are embodied in diagnostic control systems. Autonomous strategic behavior focuses on initiatives outside the scope of the current strategy, which can lead senior managers to recognize that major changes in strategy are necessary.

---

[3]For a review of organizational learning, see Levitt and March (1988).

In the induced strategic process, top management's role is to ensure the pursuit of an intended strategy through administrative and cultural mechanisms that couple operational-level strategic initiatives with the intended strategy. Doing so makes it possible for the organization to build on past success and to exploit the opportunities associated with the current domain. However, . . . it is important that the structural context reflect the selective pressures of the environment. This provides a reality test for the organizational strategy. In the autonomous strategic process, top management's role is strategic recognition rather that strategic planning. Top management needs to facilitate the activation of strategic context determination processes to find out which of the autonomous initiatives have adaptive value for the organization and deserve to become part of the organization's strategy. (1991, 255–56)

Burgelman proposes that successful organizations have learned how to manage induced strategic behavior and stimulate autonomous strategic behavior. In our framework, interactive control systems guide the experimentation and learning that are necessary for new autonomous strategic initiatives to emerge and be tested in the organization.

Managers probably have used these techniques for a long time, but the techniques have never been acknowledged conceptually. The following describes Alfred Sloan's use of what may have been an interactive control system in the 1930s:

Sloan's vision was so fixedly focused on the future that he geared GM's accounting system not so much to measuring past results—as was then typical—but to anticipating and shaping future performances. "By means of our accounting system," he noted, "we can look forward . . . and can alter our procedures or policies to the end that a better operation may result." Thus the [control system] designers changed emphasis from determining past or current performance with feedback information to predicting future performance with . . . data on environmental conditions, particularly consumer decision states. Brown [who was charged with designing and implementing these systems] separated these . . . efforts into short-term and long-term factors. Short-term factors of influence on demand were those that could "quickly be called into play to offset unfavorable developments. They include special sales stimulus, more intensive advertising, or even temporary underpricing, whenever these seem called for by a falling off in anticipated and logical demand." The long term . . . effects include "those relating to consumer appeal in style, functioning, serviceability, etc." Here, "engineers and salesmen work hand in hand" in order to improve the probabilities of consumer acceptance. (Kuhn 1986, 210)

Design Considerations

In the examples given earlier, senior managers at a soft drink company chose to use a market-share monitoring system interactively; those at a national newspaper chose a "Friday Packet," those at a health-care supply company chose a project monitoring system. How did they choose? What criteria do senior managers use in determining the system or systems to use interactively?

Five conditions are necessary for any control system to be a candidate for use as an interactive control system.

1. To be used interactively, the control system must require the reforecasting of future states based on revised current information. An interactive control system focuses attention on patterns of change; the critical questions asked by managers are, "What has changed and why?" To trigger these questions, continual reforecasting of future states, based on a reevaluation of current information, is necessary. As in a diagnostic system, actual results are compared with expectations, but any significant discrepancy—positive or negative—triggers a search for understanding. Changes evident in the data warn participants to anticipate patterns of potential change in the future. Missing a target because of a competitor's introduction of a new product triggers a reforecasting of competitive conditions. An understanding of changed conditions allows participants to estimate the potential effects on current plans, goals, and strategies and forces a dialogue about the underlying causes.

2. To be used interactively, the information contained in a control system must be simple to understand. To generate understanding, learning, and revised action plans, debate must focus on the causes and implications of information rather than on how the information was constructed and reported. Market-share data, for example, are simple to understand. Elaborate cost accounting systems based on activity-based costing and two-stage indirect cost allocations are not. Complex systems that rely on complicated transformations of data by staff experts cannot be used interactively. Managers will have little confidence in their understanding or the validity of the underlying data. Moreover, information from complex systems often suffers from collection and processing delays.

3. To be used interactively, a control system must be used not only by senior managers but also by managers at multiple levels of the organization. To serve as a catalyst for search activities, the system must be useful and widely used by a broad array of participants. This condition is met by a profit plan; it is not met by a long-range strategic plan.

4. To be used interactively, a control system must trigger revised action plans. After discussing and understanding what has changed and why, the critical question becomes, "What are we going to do about it? How can we respond to these threats or exploit these circumstances?"

Recall the analogy to the data collection system used by the national weather service: when significant patterns in weather become discernible, the benefit derives from action. In competitive situations, forecasts of changing conditions must provide significant input on how to adjust strategy to gain advantage. This type of information is vital to organizations that want to encourage participants to test new ideas and strategies and adapt in competitive markets.

The four conditions listed above are necessary, but not sufficient, conditions for senior managers to use a control system interactively. The fifth condition is critical.

5. To be used interactively, a control system must collect and generate information that relates to the effects of strategic uncertainties on the strategy of the business. As discussed earlier, strategic uncertainties are unique to specific industries and the business strategies chosen by each competitor and, therefore, will be uniquely determined for each business.

A study of thirty businesses in the U.S. health-care products industry indicated that senior managers in this industry typically chose to use one of the following five control systems interactively (Simons 1991):

1. project management systems—systems that monitor discrete blocks of organizational activity, usually on a project basis. Critical path analyses, Gantt charts, and other types of milestone planning and analysis are used in these systems.
2. profit planning systems—financial systems that report planned and actual revenues and expenses for each business by revenue and cost category. Examples include annual profit plans or budgets, second-year forecasts, and strategic operating and financial plans.
3. brand revenue budgets—systems that focus exclusively on revenue by brand, including unit volume and price by segment, type of packaging, and promotional campaigns. Market share data and shipment data are also included in these systems.
4. intelligence systems—systems that gather and disseminate information about social, political, and technical business environments. Data bases are compiled from industry reports, legislative group filings, scientific and trade journals, and annual reports of competitors.

5. human development systems—systems that establish an inventory of skills and management potential and monitor the development plans of selected employees. These systems include long-range strategic manpower systems, management-by-objectives systems, career planning and counselling systems, and succession planning systems.

Figure 5.5 illustrates the relationship between business strategy, strategic uncertainties, and interactive control systems in the health-care products industry.

Choosing Which Systems to Use Interactively

The design features of any interactive control system—the types of measures used, the system focus, and the planning horizon—depend on such factors as the business technology; the degree of government regulation and protection; the complexity of the value chain; and the ease of tactical response by competitors.

Exhibit 5.2 highlights how these factors influence the design and choice of interactive management control systems in various types of firms:

Technological dependence. Some product markets are highly dependent on a given set of technologies. Businesses competing in these markets are forced to follow technological developments in the field carefully. The more dependent a business or industry segment is on a given technology base, the more imperative it becomes for managers to protect their competitive advantage or disrupt the advantage of competitors by focusing attention on new ways of applying technology. In these cases, interactive project management systems may be most effective. On the other hand, where technological dependence is low or diversified across products—customers tend not to be locked to any one product concept—senior managers must focus attention on finding unique ways of responding to customer needs through new products or new ways of marketing existing products. In these cases, interactive brand revenue systems or interactive profit planning systems may be useful.

Regulation. Managers operating in regulated industries, such as public utilities and research-based pharmaceutical companies must

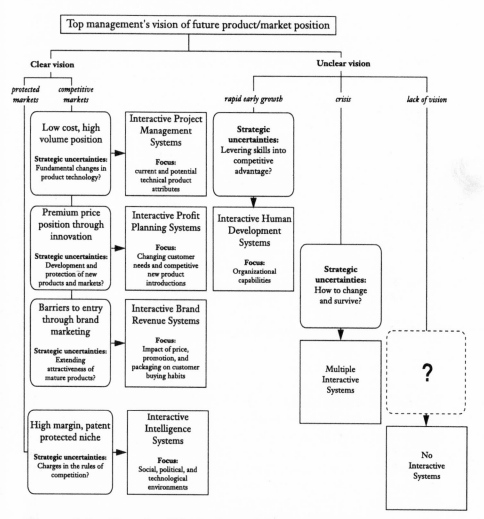

Figure 5.5 Choosing Which Control System to Use Interactively in the Health Care Products Industry

Determinant	If Determinant is HIGH, then Interactive Control System	If Determinant is LOW, then Interactive Control System
Technological Dependence	Focuses on emerging new technologies	Focuses on changing customer needs
Regulation and Market Protection	Focuses on sociopolitical threats and opportunities	Focuses on competitive threats and opportunities
Value Chain Complexity	Uses accounting-based measures	Uses input/output unit-based measures
Ease of Tactical Response	Uses short planning horizon	Uses long planning horizon

Exhibit 5.2 Factors Affecting the Design of Interactive Control Systems

pay special attention to public sentiment, political pressures, and emerging regulations and legislation. For these firms, interactive intelligence systems become important for gathering data to understand and influence, when possible, the complex social, political, and technical environments of their businesses.

Value chain complexity. Managers of businesses with complex value chains, for example, those with ongoing product innovation in multiple markets, must monitor trade-offs across product lines and markets. In these businesses, inputs, production, distribution, and sales and marketing tend to be linked in complex and dynamic ways. Therefore, for these businesses, accounting-based measures, such as interactive profit planning systems, can provide essential indicators of threats and opportunities because these systems highlight the effects of altering combinations of variables. By contrast, managers of businesses with stable, well-understood value chains, for example, mature consumer brands, have fewer complex trade-offs to manage. They can, therefore, reduce the level of complexity by focusing attention on simpler input and output measures, such as brand volume and share. These businesses often use brand revenue budget systems interactively.

Ease of tactical response. If copying a competitor's tactics is easy, the planning horizon is extremely short. Tactical responsiveness, rather than planning, becomes the key to winning, and interactive brand revenue budgeting systems permit this. If emulating the strategic initiative of competitors is difficult due to technological or market constraints, planning horizons are longer and interactive program management systems or interactive profit planning systems are effective (Simons, 1991).

Consider, for example, Johnson & Johnson, which competes with a premium price position and high levels of product innovation. Johnson & Johnson uses its profit planning system interactively to focus attention on strategic uncertainties related to the development and protection of new products and markets. Periodically during the year, Johnson & Johnson managers reestimate the predicted effects of competitive tactics and new product roll-outs on their profit plans for the current and following year. They also adjust five and ten year plans. The recurring questions posed by managers are, "What has changed since our last forecast? Why? What are we going to do about it?" (Simons 1987b, 1987c).

Reference to Exhibit 5.2 suggests that their choice of an interactive profit planning system makes sense. The technological dependence of the business is low, suggesting that the interactive system should focus on changing customer needs; there is little government regulation in most parts of its business, so the system can be designed to focus on competitive threats and opportunities; the emphasis on innovation and product diversity results in high value chain complexity, suggesting the appropriateness of accounting-based measures to monitor trade-offs; and the ease of tactical response by competitors is intermediate, indicating the need for a planning horizon longer than weeks but shorter than years.

Risks in Choosing the Wrong Interactive Control System

It is important to understand that the control system used interactively in one firm may be used diagnostically in another. Senior managers determine where participants should focus attention. A project management system used interactively will focus attention on fundamental changes in product technology; an interactive brand revenue system will focus attention on the impact of price, promotion, and packaging on customer buying habits; an interactive profit planning system will focus attention on changing customer needs and competitive new product introductions. Any choice, of course, entails the risk of error. In the case of interactive control systems, the error may

focus organizational search on the wrong strategic uncertainties. By
guiding an organization's search behavior, interactive control systems
may divert organizational attention from cues that would enable successful adaptation. By focusing attention on subsets of potential opportunity within that space, other opportunities are eliminated from
consideration.

Managers at a large integrated oil company used an interactive
project management system to focus attention on reserve reports,
competitive bidding plans, and exploration proposals. The system
was used as a catalyst to develop coherent exploration strategies and
organizational capabilities. When oil prices dropped precipitously,
managers continued to focus attention on the project management
systems and related exploration strategies, assuming that oil prices
would recover. A crisis ensued that resulted ultimately in the removal
of senior managers.[4]

Why Strategic Planning Can Never Be an Interactive System

It is sometimes assumed that strategic planning can become a good
interactive system because strategic planning should focus on strategic
uncertainties and should involve senior managers. However, long-
range planning systems are not used throughout the organization and
are not linked to revised action plans. Therefore, strategic planning
systems cannot be used as interactive systems.

During the 1970s strategic planning was hailed as a technique
that would revolutionize management. Strategic planners were hired,
professional planning associations were formed, and strategic planning departments were created in many leading companies. Fifteen
years later, the planners are gone, and the departments disbanded or
reduced dramatically in size. Although the failures of strategic planning are usually attributed to a lack of senior management commitment and involvement (Steiner 1979, 293; Lorange 1980, 258), I
believe the real reason for the failure lies in a fundamental misunder-
standing of the relationship between strategic planning and control.
Strategic planning has been defined as a means to formulate strategies
(Anthony 1988, 30–34). Staff planners have been notorious in their

[4]From a paper prepared by Mark Gallion for the Harvard M.B.A. course Strategic
Management Systems, 1989.

attempts to cajole senior managers into using long-range planning systems interactively, but managers have uniformly refused to commit the necessary attention to strategic planning to make the system interactive. Why? Because strategic planning is a system for implementing strategy, not formulating strategy (Mintzberg 1994, 239, 333). New strategies are rarely, if ever, arrived at through formal planning. Detailed planning, whether short-term or long-term, whether done in staff offices or off-site at a retreat, is primarily a tool of implementation. It is a process of formalizing the ideas already percolating in the minds of managers to ensure that the resources are on hand for successful execution.

The traditional view of strategic planning and control associates strategic planning with strategy formation and control with implementation. But this puts the cart before the horse. Strategic planning is a diagnostic control tool. New strategic initiatives are not developed through strategic planning but rather through interactive controls that guide the development of new strategic initiatives within the constraints provided by boundary systems. Thus, the framework developed here inverts the traditional relationship and equates interactive control with strategy formation and strategic planning with implementation (Figure 5.6).

In setting strategic boundaries and fostering daily interaction around business problems and opportunities, control systems have as much to do with strategy formation as they have to do with strategy implementation. The same cannot be said for strategic planning.

*Choosing How Many Control Systems
to Use Interactively*

In normal competitive conditions, senior managers with a clear sense of strategic vision choose very few—usually only one—management control systems to use interactively at any point in time (Simons 1990). Managers use only one system for three reasons: economic, cognitive, and strategic.

In economic terms, interactive control systems are costly. Managers must balance multiple tasks and roles. Decision making and control occupy only a subset of a manager's day-to-day activities (Mintzberg 1973, 166–70). By definition, interactive control systems demand frequent attention throughout the organization and therefore exact high opportunity costs by diverting attention from other tasks.

Traditional
View

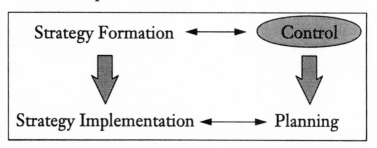

Revised
Relationships

Figure 5.6   Inverting the Relationship Between Planning
and Control

In cognitive terms, the ability of individuals to process large
amounts of disparate information is limited. Decision makers suffer
from information overload as the amount and complexity of information is increased (Schroder, Driver, Streufert 1967, 36). Using too
many systems interactively overburdens the organization as individuals are unable to process the data necessary to support the dialogue
and debate that fuels the interactive process.

In strategic terms, the primary reason for using a control system
interactively is to activate learning and experimentation. Attempting
to focus intensively on too many management control systems at the
same time risks information overload, superficial analysis, a lack of
perspective, and potential paralysis. Managers of firms in crisis typi-

cally use all control systems interactively for the short period necessary to figure out how to change and survive. But there is a limit to the organization's energy and attention. Intensive focus on all systems simultaneously causes incredible stress as employees are pushed to their limits to respond to the short-term information and action demands of superiors. Furthermore using multiple systems interactively diffuses senior management's signals of strategic uncertainties because attention is dispersed over several areas.

Senior managers must also determine when to change the focus of interactive control systems. As competitive conditions and senior management vision changes, strategic uncertainties also change. In the case of the integrated oil company discussed earlier, a new strategy of maximizing reserve potentials resulted in using profit planning as a new interactive control system. A change in strategy should result in a change in the interactive control systems. Waiting too long to redefine which systems will be used interactively can cause an organization to become out of step with emerging opportunities. Innovation and adaptation will suffer. On the other hand, changing signals too often can send conflicting signals and cause confusion and lack of focus in the organization.

Senior managers without a strategic vision (or an urgency to create a strategic vision) do not use control systems interactively. A lack of vision seems to be associated with a lack of identifiable interactive control systems in organizations. More important, a lack of vision represents a lack of strategic leadership and bodes poorly for the ability of the firm to be a successful competitor in its markets (Simons 1991).

Interactive Control Systems and Formal Incentives

For a control system to be truly interactive, there must be specially designed incentives. Rewards for achievement in the activities monitored by an interactive control system are not determined by formula. Interactive control systems are associated with subjective, contribution-based rewards. There are two aspects of this proposition to be considered: subjectivity in the reward structure and rewarding contribution rather than results.

Rewards are *subjective* when superiors make personal judgments based on both fact and intuition as to the appropriate level of reward for participants. Subjective rewards allow managers to recognize innovative behavior that is difficult, if not impossible, to specify *ex ante* and/or to measure *ex post*. By its very nature, innovation relies on individual opportunity-seeking. Creativity is the outcome that is valued. Managers cannot, therefore, prespecify what specific outcomes will be rewarded. Subjective rewards provide the necessary flexibility to acknowledge the contribution and effort expended in creative search behavior, testing new ideas, and sharing information throughout the organization. Johnson & Johnson uses subjective rewards to recognize contributions captured by their interactive profit planning systems; Turner Construction uses subjective rewards to recognize contribution captured by their interactive project monitoring system.

Rewarding contribution rather than results stimulates organizational learning. Because rewards are not tied to environmental conditions beyond the control of participants, the rewards encourage information sharing, new action plans, and learning. Participants are more likely to share environmental predictions, for example, worsening demand conditions, because changes in these exogenous variables will not affect their rewards.

Furthermore, when contribution is rewarded, participants attempt to make their efforts visible to superiors. For managerial work, effort and contribution are inherently difficult to observe. Under subjective reward schemes, participants communicate information about problems and opportunities they have encountered, as well as action plans they have implemented or proposed, in order to demonstrate to superiors their efforts and contributions. This enhances the learning-related benefits of interactive systems. For these reasons, control systems *cannot* be used interactively if incentives are linked by formula to fixed, *ex ante* goals. As discussed in the previous chapter, linking rewards to results by formula invites gamesmanship and bias.

Finally, to assign subjective awards equitably, superiors must have a sound understanding of the business environment, decision context, array of possible alternatives, and potential outcomes of actions not taken. Rewards can be determined fairly only if managers understand the contribution of participants in specific circumstances. Although participants supply some of this information as part of their ongoing interactive dialogue, the more fundamental knowledge of opportunity space and cause-effect relationships must come from a senior manager's deep understanding of the business. Thus, the use of interactive control systems requires senior managers with intimate business and industry knowledge. This condition can be fulfilled most easily by promoting from within or by hiring only those outsiders with deep industry knowledge.

Strong business experience brings additional benefits. First, organizational learning is enhanced through the increased quality of the questioning and debate generated by senior managers. Second, participants perceive the subjective reward system as legitimate because senior managers really understand the efforts and contributions made. Finally, senior managers who have been promoted through the ranks or have come to the company through a similar career path elsewhere are alert for and minimize any undesirable behavior or gaming that may result from the use of subjective rewards.

Subjective rewards can be both economic and noneconomic. Economic rewards relate to current purchasing power—salary and cash bonuses—and to future purchasing power—stock options. But, praise and recognition can provide powerful noneconomic rewards that lead to feelings of prestige and self-worth. Effective managers use praise and recognition liberally and publicly to reward the individual risk-taking and opportunity-seeking related to interactive control systems.

Promotion, which brings economic benefit, recognition, and prestige, is the final category of reward. Promotion is an important ingredient of rewarding individual contributions to debate and dialogue for two reasons. First, interactive processes highlight each individual's ability to create goals, meaning, and action plans independent of outside direction. This is an important determinant of an individual's readiness to take on greater organizational responsibility. Second, interactive processes expose each individual's skill in identifying and shaping strategic uncertainties, a necessary prerequisite for higher level positions in the firm.

Profit Planning as a Special Case

The use of profit planning, which is the prototypical diagnostic control system in many firms, as an interactive control system presents a special case that sheds additional light on the design of incentives for interactive systems in general. To follow the line of reasoning presented above, a profit planning system would, if used interactively, be linked to subjective, effort-based rewards.[5] Bonus payouts, for example, would not be determined solely by reference to a preset formula; instead, bonuses would be determined by a senior manager's subjective judgment about how well participants have performed in the circumstances. Results below initial expectations might be rewarded if subordinates were able to demonstrate that they had performed well in an unexpectedly difficult market, or, results above expectations might be discounted if some fortuitous event led to higher performance.

Given the conditions described in Exhibit 5.2, a firm might use its profit planning system interactively when it has a complex value chain, a diverse technology base, and competes in highly competitive, unregulated markets. In these situations, profit planning provides a simple, easily updated framework to discuss changes in competitive markets, the business effects of changing the value chain equation, and the anticipated effects of new action plans and competitor reactions. For a certain subset of firms, then, the use of profit planning as an interactive system is appropriate. Even for these firms, however, profit targets must yield results that are acceptable to stockholders and others with an economic interest in the firm. Profit plans, then, must be used both diagnostically and interactively. How can managers accomplish this?

The solution is suggested by the following proposition: interactive control systems have contingency buffers added to protect key diagnostic targets. Contingencies provide an escape valve that allows constructive dialogue and ensures that key targets are not jeopardized. In the case of profit planning, consider first how a traditional diagnostic profit plan might be handled. A senior manager may negotiate with corporate superiors that the business will deliver $10 million in profits in the next year. In a stable, noninnovative business, this figure becomes a fixed commitment that is incorporated in the business's profit plan. The $10 million target can be allocated across divisions and monitored periodically in a typical diagnostic fashion. Incentives can be tied by formula to the profit plan target without the use of a contingency buffer.

In a highly competitive, innovative business, however, senior

---

[5] This echoes the result of Govindarajin and Gupta (1985) who noted in their study of fifty-eight strategic business units in eight diversified firms that growing, innovative businesses were more likely to use subjective rewards than were businesses that were being run for cash flow and ultimate decline.

managers may wish to use the firm's profit planning system more interactively to create pressure for innovation and focus attention on strategic uncertainties. Rather than treating the profit goal as a fixed target, the interactive profit planning process would require bottom-up revision of the profit goal periodically, based on changing circumstances. In this case, the senior manager might build in a contingency that would hold participants accountable for an initial target of $11 million with a $1 million contingency fund that could be drawn upon, after mutual agreement, if they were unable to meet their target. Monthly meetings would discuss achievement against the profit plan, reasons for under- or over-performance, revised estimates based on new product roll-outs and competitor actions, and proposed action plans.

By mutual agreement, profit plan targets would be adjusted during the year and the contingency could be drawn upon if needed to protect the key target of $10 million. Incentives could be determined subjectively based on innovative efforts to expand and seize new opportunities to meet the $11 million goal; the contingency fund could be used as a buffer if necessary to ensure that at least $10 million is achieved. Both Johnson & Johnson and Turner Construction use this approach.

Roles for Managers and Staff Groups

Diagnostic control systems act as attention-conserving devices for senior managers: they allow businesses to operate without constant monitoring. For diagnostic control systems, then, staff groups act as gatekeepers, maintainers, and system experts.

Interactive control systems are attention enhancers. Senior managers use these systems intensively and frequently. As a result, managers throughout the organization assume primary responsibility for shaping the data in a way that is most useful to them and for interpreting and working with the information contained in the system. These tasks are not delegated. Staff groups are used primarily as facilitators in the interactive process. They assist in the gathering, collating, and distribution of data and facilitate the meetings in which business managers debate and discuss action plans. The objective is to keep the interactive system simple and accessible to operating managers to ensure that it is used by managers throughout the organization.

Middle managers are especially important in making the interactive control process work effectively. Middle managers are key nodes of the information network that reveals senior management's concerns and moves newly collected information up, down, and sideways in the organization. Japanese scholar Ikujiro Nonaka describes their importance:

The entrepreneurial middle must confront and survive the criticism of the other members of the group through intensive communication. An idea must successfuly challenge the stability of the organization, involving people from the top and bottom, left and right. As the organization moves in the direction of innovation, creative chaos is amplified to focus on specific contradictions in order to solve the problem. These contradictions produce a demand for a new perspective, speeding up information creation activity. This approach is exemplified by the Honda R&D manager's statement, "Creativity is born by pushing people against the wall and pressuring them almost to the extreme." (1988, 15)

Managing an interactive control system is a delicate task. Senior managers must use these systems to build internal pressure and to gather information and develop action plans. A senior executive at a Turner Construction Company described his use of an interactive project monitoring system,

I try to be a devil's advocate, looking for problems and being suspicious. I get four reports each month—one for each territory. But before they are finalized, I go to each territory and sit down with the Territory General Manager and his staff to go over problems and opportunities. A lot of discussion focuses on the proper level for contingencies.

You must have a contingency as an escape route. That is why it is so important to discuss these things face-to-face. With his boss sitting there, I can look a young cost engineer in the eye and ask, "Can we save $300,000 on this job?" I can read his eyes and I know the answer. When I sit down with Gary and Jayne, I look for the eyes to go from one to the other when I ask the tough questions. (Simons and Weston 1990d, 9)

This process can be threatening. Using control systems interactively to trigger learning requires an environment that values openness and accepts constructive challenge and debate. Without due care, participants in the interactive control process may feel threatened by the active interest and participation of senior managers. The threat of embarrassment can subvert learning. Participants may feel at risk as the quality of their effort and thinking is challenged publicly. Autonomy may be threatened with an attendant reduction in risk taking. Participants may be afraid to challenge the assumptions and action plans of their peers and senior managers, which can result in defensive behavior. The meetings chaired by Harold Geneen at ITT were notorious for the consequences that befell the unprepared.

Argyris has studied extensively the factors that lead individuals and organizations to create defensive routines, which he defines as the policies or actions that are intended to circumvent embarrassment or threat by bypassing situations that may trigger these responses (Argyris 1990a, 505). Chernobyl again provides a grim example:

When Khenokh [director of the nuclear power station] said that one of the units at his power station would not be ready in time because of delays in the delivery of equipment, Shcerbina [deputy premier with responsibility for energy] exploded: "You see, what a hero! He sets his own deadlines." And then he shouted, "Who gave you the right, comrade Khenokh, to establish your own deadlines in place of the government's?" After the meeting, Khenokh remarked sadly . . . "We ourselves tell lies and teach our subordinates to lie. A lie even with a noble purpose is still a lie. And no good will come of it." (Holloway 1990, 5)

Nonproductive, defensive behaviors include failing to challenge unreasoned statements, blocking diversity in opinion, echoing the views of superiors in a desire to please, communicating in ambiguous and inconsistent ways, and making these failures of communication and learning undiscussable (Argyris 1990b). Senior managers must ensure that these types of behavior do not subvert the learning the interactive control process is designed to stimulate. Effective managers must reward and encourage those willing to dissent, take risks, share information, and propose novel ideas.

Summary

To summarize the distinctive features of interactive control systems and how they are managed, a comparison with the attributes of diagnostic control systems is presented in Exhibit 5.3. The common denominator for all interactive control systems is continuous reestimation of future states and consideration of how to best react. Interactive systems are not only concerned with forecasting but, more important, with linking forecasts to action. Attention to process, rather than to predetermined outcomes, is the critical ingredient of success.

	Business Strategy	
	↙	↘
Strategy as . . .	Target	Vision
Focus	Critical Performance Variables	Strategic Uncertainties
	↓	↓
	Diagnostic Control Systems	*Interactive Control Systems*
Purpose	Provide motivation and direction to achieve goals	Stimulate dialogue and organizational learning
Goal	No surprises	Creative search
Analytical reasoning	Deductive (flying by instrument)	Inductive, sensory (flying by feel)
System complexity	Complex	Simple
Time Frame	Past and present	Present and future
Targets	Fixed	Constantly reestimated
Feedback	Negative feedback	Positive feedback
Adjustment to	Inputs or process	Double loop learning
Communication	Eliminate need for talk	Provide common language
Staff role	Key gatekeepers	Facilitators

Exhibit 5.3   A Comparison of Diagnostic and Interactive Control Systems

PART III

A Dynamic Framework
for Controlling Business Strategy

CHAPTER 6

The Control Levers in Action

Now that each lever has been described in detail, we can examine how managers pick and choose among them to implement their strategic agendas. Control systems are not equal in either timing or purpose. They evolve to meet the information and control needs of individual managers and their organizations. To understand this, consider a simplified overview of how control systems are implemented over the life cycle of the firm (Figure 6.1).

In the start-up phase, there is little demand for formal control systems. Because employees are in constant face-to-face communication with each other, it is possible to control key aspects of the business without formal reporting structures. Internal accounting controls to ensure that assets are secure and accounting information is reliable are the only formal control systems needed.

In the growth stage, however, increasing size requires that more decision-making authority be delegated to lower levels. As a result, formal, measurable goals and the monitoring of participants' activities become increasingly important. Diagnostic control systems are implemented for the first time to meet the information and control needs of senior managers. Performance incentives are tied to the achievement of diagnostic targets.

This chapter is adapted from Robert Simons, "How New Top Managers Use Control Systems as Levers of Strategic Renewal," *Strategic Management Journal* 15 (1994):169–89. Copyright © 1994 by John Wiley & Sons, Ltd. Reprinted by permission of John Wiley & Sons, Ltd.

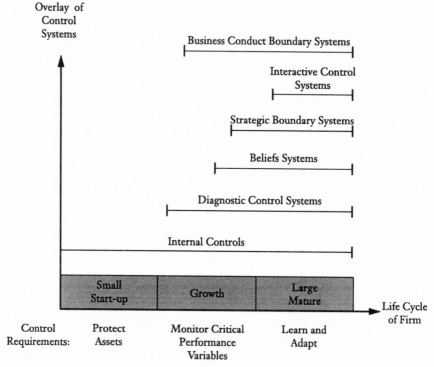

Figure 6.1 Evolution of Management Control Systems over the Life Cycle of the Firm

By the end of the growth phase, the company operates in multiple markets with a variety of locations. At this stage, a formal beliefs system is implemented. Mission and vision statements are created and communicated to motivate, empower, and supply direction. At the same time, managers learn that certain types of activities should be declared off-limits. Bad investments and failed projects result in new strategic boundaries that delimit opportunity space.

In mature firms, senior managers learn to rely on the opportunity-seeking behavior of subordinates for innovation and new strategic initiatives. At this stage, they begin to use selected control systems interactively. Beliefs systems, strategic boundaries, diagnostic control systems, and interactive control systems now work together to control the formation and implementation of strategy. Finally, business conduct boundaries are imposed any time that a crisis demonstrates the costs of errant employee actions.

In this simplified picture, control levers are static and lifeless. The picture fails to reveal the power and timing of techniques employed by managers to maintain or alter patterns in organizational activities. How do managers use these levers to implement their agendas? What are the pressure points to influence the behavior of subordinates? What is the ebb and flow of managerial attention to the different control systems? To provide insight into how control systems influence behaviors and drive strategic renewal, the remainder of this chapter describes the results of a study of ten newly appointed managers and their use of the four control levers.

How Ten New Senior Managers Use the Levers of Control

"Systems is our most critical gap. Without proper systems to integrate the data, it will be very hard to make our strategy work."

The managers were newly appointed company presidents who reported either to a board of directors or to parent company executives. By focusing on new managers, the research capitalizes on situations of change as a way of exploring the causal relationships between strategy and the levers of control. Since past research suggests that insiders and outsiders may vary in the degree of organizational change that they implement, the sample was split to include five managers who were promoted from within the organization and five who were recruited externally.[1]

The ten managers and their organizations are described in Exhibit 6.1. The size and nature of their organizations varied significantly, but the way in which each used the control levers to drive change was remarkably similar.

The research tracked the ten managers for the first eighteen months of their tenures. Each agreed to be interviewed and to supply data at four month intervals to document their agendas, action plans, and use of formal systems. Subordinates were also interviewed to help interpret the nature and magnitude of change. Data on personal background, experience, and reasons for succession were collected. Organizational changes in strategy, structure, and process were documented. Copies of formal documents relating to planning and control

---

[1] For a discussion of the differential effects of insiders and outsiders, see Wiersema (1992) and Helmich and Brown (1972).

Business	Unit Revenues (millions $)	Title	Immediate Superior	Insider (I) or Outsider (O) to Organization
Computer Manufacturer	2,000	President	Parent Company Executive	I
Bank	2,000	President	Parent Company Executive	I
Can Manufacturer	4,000	President	Parent Company Executive	O
Machinery Manufacturer	350	President	Parent Company Executive	I
Food Manufacturer	400	President	Parent Company Executive	O
Branded Consumer Products	6,000	President	Board of Directors (and retiring CEO during transition)	I
Electric Utility	1,800	President	Board of Directors	O
Health Aids	600	President	Board of Directors	O
Paper Manufacturer	2,800	President	Retiring CEO and Board of Directors	O
Retail Manufacturer and Merchant	2,700	President	Board of Directors	I

Exhibit 6.1 Description of Newly Appointed Top Managers and Their Businesses

systems were gathered. In addition, public data were gathered during the period, including press coverage, analysts' reports, and annual reports.

All ten managers in the sample actively used management control systems to promote and support strategic change. The sample bifurcated, however, into two distinct clusters according to the mandate for change perceived by each of the managers. The first cluster was made up of four managers who were implementing revolutionary change. These managers and their organizations were classified as Cluster 1: Strategic Turnaround. The other six managers were taking over situations that required some change, but their role was to maintain the success and momentum of the business. These managers and their organizations are classified as Cluster 2: Strategic Evolution. Exhibit 6.2 illustrates the history and strategic success of each firm.

I had anticipated that managers hired from outside the firm would be more likely to institute revolutionary change than those promoted from within, but the data did not support this conclusion. Two of the four managers in Cluster 1 were external hires; two were promoted internally. Of the six managers in Cluster 2, three were external recruits and three were internal promotions.

Over the eighteen-month period, these managers and their subordinates were asked repeatedly to describe how and why formal control systems were used: How much time was allocated to each system? How and why did the focus of attention change? Where did the initiative for change originate? Who participated in substantive issues such as goal setting, incentive compensation formula, development of new missions and strategies, and planning guidelines and targets? What was the pace and order of these interventions? What were the respective roles for senior managers and staff groups in these processes? What aspects were delegated and what aspects were handled personally by senior managers?

Cluster 1: Strategic Turnaround

"Time is what keeps me awake at night. We have burned our currency. We abused our marketplace. We let them down on expectations and delivered a poor quality product."

Each manager in this cluster was redirecting the basic strategy of the business. In three of the four businesses, the mandate for change was provided by the failure of past strategies that had at-

	Results of Past Strategy	Past Top Manager	New Top Manager
Strategic Turnaround Cluster			
Computer Manufacturer	Unsuccessful niche strategy; Market failure and heavy losses	Terminated	Internally promoted
Bank	Unsuccessful diversification; Bad loans and heavy losses	Terminated	Internally promoted
Food Manufacturer	Stuck in the middle; unexploited potential	Terminated	Outsider
Health Aids	Franchise eroded; failed diversification	Terminated	Outsider
Strategic Evolution Cluster			
Can Manufacturer	High-volume, low-cost market leader	Resigned after corporate acquisition	Outsider
Machinery Manufacturer	Market leader in niche	Retired	Internally promoted
Branded Consumer Products	Market leader with strong brand franchises	Still chairman; in transition	Internally promoted
Electric Utility	Innovative monopoly in regulated environment	Died unexpectedly	Outsider
Paper Manufacturer	Market leader in niche	In transition	Outsider
Retail Manufacturer/Merchant	Market leader in niche	Still chairman; in transition	Internally promoted

Exhibit 6.2 Strategic History of Sample Companies

tempted to build new niche markets, expand geographically, or diversify into new product markets. These failures had resulted in significant financial losses. Three of the managers were replacing managers who had been displaced as a result of failed strategies. In the fourth business, the new manager had been hired externally by a corporate parent that had recently acquired the business. This manager was asked to provide a new strategic focus and build up the scale of the business, which had been underperforming.

Managers of turnaround situations are usually under pressure to improve performance (Gabarro 1987, 51). Because of the urgency communicated by superiors, these managers realized they would not last if short-term problems were not overcome (as the chairman of an international conglomerate told one of the managers, "Welcome to the fast lane. But you should know that if you don't keep accelerating, you will be run over").

Each manager spent the first several months reviewing and appraising opportunities for the business. Although all the managers travelled to various business locations, met with subordinates, suppliers, and customers, and initiated in-depth economic analyses to better understand strategic options, little substantive change was implemented during this three-month period. Three of the managers created in-house consulting task forces to analyze markets dynamics, competitive threats, and potential opportunities. One manager used external consultants to develop a data base to analyze markets, test organizational capabilities, and perform competitor analyses.[2]

For the first twelve months of their tenures, managers perceived three urgent demands:

- overcoming organizational inertia
- structuring and communicating performance expectations
- gaining organizational allegiance to the new agenda

The use of formal systems played an important role in meeting all three of these demands.

Using Management Control Systems to Overcome Organizational Inertia

"I keep telling my people that carrying on doing the same thing is unacceptable."

Managers engineering strategic turnaround receive a mandate to change the organization in fundamental ways. Yet, organizations pos-

---

[2]Gabarro (1987), pp. 20–24, discusses this orientation/evaluation stage in detail.

sess considerable inertia that must be overcome if substantive change is to be introduced and sustained (Miller and Friesen 1984, ch. 10). Habit, standard operating procedures, and programs in progress promote stable behavior patterns among longstanding groups (Hannan and Freeman 1984; Nelson and Winter 1982, ch. 5). To implement a new agenda, managers must create momentum in a new direction, but first, old behaviors must be unlearned (Argyris 1985, 274).

To do this, organizations frequently replace key individuals whose behaviors and attitudes do not align with the new strategy (Tushman, Newman, and Romanelli 1987). All four managers replaced direct subordinates in several key jobs. In three of the companies, for example, the chief financial officer, marketing vice president, and international vice president were replaced.

Because it is neither feasible nor desirable to replace the entire organization, all four managers instead used beliefs systems and boundary systems to create impetus for the new, emerging agenda and to demarcate the domain for new strategic initiatives. As the new strategy for the business became clear (within the first six months), all four managers personally drafted new mission statements for their businesses. These statements were written between the third and sixth months of their tenure. The statements addressed core beliefs, target markets, and identified core product categories. The statements presented, in very broad terms, the new manager's agenda for the organization. For example, the new mission statement of one company that was embarking on an ambitious global expansion strategy was simply "To firmly establish our brands as the world's undisputed leader in our various markets." The manager of another company in which a failed diversification strategy had allowed a strong brand franchise to erode wrote the mission statement reproduced in Exhibit 6.3.

All the mission statements were couched in inspirational language to supply fresh energy and motivation to the organization. Exhibit 6.3 illustrates the phrasing used by these managers: "We will exert great effort . . . continuous improvement . . . low cost producer . . . high product quality . . . makes us burst with pride." As one manager stated, "Growth is our number one goal, so we must inspire as well as manage." The beliefs systems created by these managers were intentionally vague so they could appeal to individuals at all levels of the organization.

Formal boundary systems that clearly specified types of behavior no longer tolerated counterbalanced the inspirational beliefs systems.

Mission

1. Our objective is to be the leading supplier in each market we serve on a worldwide basis. We will exert great effort to expand our product categories worldwide.

2. We will accomplish our share and market growth objectives through continuous improvement to our products and through product line extensions, utilizing innovative techniques of manufacturing, marketing, distribution and education that are appropriate to local conditions.

3. We will be the low cost producer in every market in which we compete, while maintaining our traditional high product quality. We will conduct all aspects of our business at a level that makes us burst with pride.

4. Diversification opportunities must build on our existing strengths and/or hold the potential for near-term profitability. Unless we can see a measurable benefit to our shareholders, we will not diversify. Rather, we will operate our basic business profitably for the shareholder.

Exhibit 6.3   Mission Statement

All four managers made it clear through planning guidelines and other formal systems that business based on the prior strategy would no longer be acceptable. More specifically, each manager formalized and communicated definite strategic boundaries. For example:

> "We will not undertake any activities that do not fit our four families of products."
> "We will not expend any resources on developing low-fat products."
> "We will no longer offer period-end promotions to boost volume."
> "Profit—*not volume*—will be our creed."

Because these boundaries precluded the pursuit of certain opportunities that had been acceptable under past management, they forced organizational participants to unlearn past behaviors. Subordinates realized failure to comply would be viewed as a serious offense when the new managers assessed which subordinates to retain and which to replace.

Each manager personally drafted documents and guidelines, wrote letters to all employees, prepared speeches and videotapes, and toured the business, conducting workshops and meetings with key subordinates. Three of the four managers also issued formal documents transmitting core values and codes of conduct. Managers referred to the documents as "rules of the road" or "corporate value statements." These beliefs systems and boundary systems attempted to inspire and constrain subordinates and break organizational inertia. Staff groups took on a new importance as they were charged with monitoring compliance.

Using Management Control Systems to Structure and Communicate Performance Expectations

"In the first year after taking over, it was tremendously important to build credibility that I could deliver results on these critical performance variables. That is why the finance function became so important and powerful for me. [The Chairman] would not have trusted us to engage in the sort of investment we are undertaking unless my fiscal performance in the first twelve months that I took over this business had been flawless."

A manager's ability to alter the direction of a business depends on continuing confidence from superiors (Warren 1984). All four managers began a focused campaign to gain the support of their relevant superiors, either a board of directors or an executive committee, between the fourth and sixth month of their tenure. Each manager presented a mission statement, discussed new strategies, and offered measurable goals for the subsequent four to five years as a personal commitment. Although superiors did not demand them, each manager set accountability goals and offered diagnostic control system goals to which he or she was willing to be held accountable. The purpose of these actions was to communicate, educate, signal commitment, and build confidence in the viability of the proposed strategic redirection.

Formal goals (e.g., financial targets, market share targets, new business targets) were used to communicate the proposed new strategic direction to superiors. One manager, for example, presented goals that would, over a four-year period, take the business into new geographical markets, increase sales from $375 million to over $1 billion, and increase net profit percentages from 12 percent to a range of 15 to 16 percent. To build and sustain their credibility with superiors, the achievement of these objectives became tremendously important for the managers. Therefore, diagnostic control systems that were capable of monitoring critical performance variables became essential. In three of the four firms, the existing diagnostic control systems were inadequate for the information and control needs of the new

managers. In each of these firms, the managers followed a dual strategy of hiring consultants to design and implement new diagnostic
control systems and recruiting a new chief financial officer to oversee
the monitoring of critical performance variables. Consultants installed
new general ledger systems, order management systems, sales reporting systems, and profit planning systems.

Each of the managers used diagnostic control systems to build
credibility through accountability both upward and downward. In all
four firms, the managers used diagnostic control systems to demand
accountability from subordinates. New and existing systems were
used to focus attention on the critical performance variables (e.g.,
number of new store openings; client accretion; operating income
reports by segment and business; cash flows) that would drive the
new strategy. One manager referred to these as "pulse measures";
another instituted a formal "report card" for subordinates and key
business functions. Diagnostic control system goals were quantitative
but not necessarily financial.

Using Management Control Systems to Gain
Organizational Allegiance to the New Agenda

*"The culture here has always been, 'If you make your financial targets, don't worry
about strategy.' I am now making it clear that if you don't hit your strategy—even
though you hit your budget—you will be penalized."*

The unwillingness of an organization to commit to a new strategy
represents a serious potential impediment for managers attempting
strategic turnaround (Greiner and Bhambri 1989). To ensure commitment to the new agendas, all four managers altered the remuneration
and incentive system for key subordinates. Base salaries for subordinate managers were increased significantly, in part to ensure equity
between newly hired replacements, who tended to be hired at higher
salary levels, and existing managers. Bonus potentials for key subordinates were also increased, but bonus incentives were linked explicitly
to the critical performance variables associated with the new strategy.
Goals were a function of critical performance variables—entry into
new markets, client accretion, store openings—not just financial success. The risk-reward function was also altered so that good performers would receive relatively more, and poor performers relatively less.

A significant proportion of bonus compensation—typically 50

percent—was changed from quantitative, formula-based measures to subjective evaluations of effort in achieving personal objectives. This subjective portion of the bonus was allocated entirely at the discretion of the four managers. By making bonuses subjective, the payout to each subordinate rested on the manager's personal assessment of the contribution, effort, and commitment to the new strategy. By making these changes, all four managers attempted to capture the attention and allegiance of subordinates.

Using Management Control Systems to Focus Attention on Strategic Uncertainties

The challenges facing all four managers changed during the second twelve months. By that time, support from superiors and senior levels of their organizations was in place, and subordinates who were unable or unwilling to commit to the new agenda had left. At this point, each manager began to focus on gaining a deeper understanding of what was required to achieve the strategic objectives that had been promised.

All four managers devoted personal attention to one control system, which, as a result, became highly interactive. The control system chosen by each top manager focused organizational attention on the strategic uncertainties associated with that manager's vision for the future. The installation of an interactive profit planning system at the health aids company illustrates the process followed by other managers.

The previous manager had used a brand revenue budgeting system interactively to focus attention on the uncertainties associated with marketing mature branded consumer products. Weekly reports that detailed market share and shipment data by category and region around the world were used to promote debate and dialogue throughout the organization in an attempt to understand how pricing, promotion, and packaging could be used to gain competitive advantage.

The new manager wished to inject more innovation into the firm's product offerings and marketing programs and hoped to direct strategy away from mature product markets. This manager wanted operating managers to use a new profit planning system interactively to promote a deeper understanding of market conditions, competitor actions, brand profitability, and the timing and effect of line extensions and new product introductions. To make this shift in emphasis visible, the manager returned the weekly brand revenue budget reports to senders with the note that he no longer wished to receive these reports for review although he expected the senders to monitor share and shipment variables. The manager and his new chief financial officer, with the help of consultants, then installed a new profit planning system that would require managers to monitor brand profitability and propose ideas for enhancing market opportunities.

Under the new system, profitability for each brand was revised and discussed from the bottom of the organization to the top on a monthly basis. Through face-to-face meetings with operating managers, the senior manager and executive committee focused attention on data from the new profit planning system and thereby sent a clear signal throughout the organization about what strategic uncertainties the organization should collect data on and respond to. Discussion centered on investment and the tactics necessary to introduce new products, develop line extensions, and enter new markets.

Similar activity occurred in the other businesses in this cluster. The manager of the bank set up an interactive control system to monitor, on a six-week basis, client growth and revenue-per-client in target markets. An interactive brand revenue budgeting system with weekly reforecasting of anticipated growth and volume targets was installed at the food manufacturer. The manager of the computer company, which was in crisis, made multiple systems interactive. In each case, a new interactive control system allowed top managers to focus organizational attention on the strategic uncertainties related to their new strategy. Exhibit 6.4 summarizes the interactive control systems and strategic uncertainties.

Revision to Strategy and Control Systems

Through the debate and dialogue generated by interactive control systems, new strategies emerged. During the second year of their tenure, all four managers refined and reinforced the vision, strategy, and formal control systems they had instituted. Changes to strategy included, for example, an acknowledgment of the new role of certain distribution outlets, better market segmentation, the introduction of new products, the sale of peripheral businesses, and the announced intention to expand into new geographical markets. Many of these changes emerged from the learning provided by the interactive control process. In three of the firms, managers held a second round of vision meetings to reaffirm and refine the vision in light of adjustments to the strategy. For example, the food manufacturer added a new product category to its mission statement after the successful testing of this

	New Strategy	New Interactive Control System	Strategic Uncertainties
Bank	Niche strategy focusing on wealthy individuals and their businesses around the world	Client-Revenue Budgeting	How is the bank and its services perceived by potential customers who demand discretion and special services?
Food Manufacturer	Innovative marketing to expand internationally	Brand-Revenue Budgeting	How can we respond to changing customer tastes and buying patterns in different countries?
Health Aids	Innovate to create new products	Profit Planning	How can we change the value equation of our narrow brand franchise to support entry into new markets?
Computer Manufacturer	Focus on value-added back office networks	Multiple	How can we survive?

Exhibit 6.4 Interactive Control Systems Used by Senior Managers in Second Twelve Months

idea in several test markets. Two of the firms reissued their value statements during this phase.

Diagnostic measurement systems were also refined, based on performance and experience over the preceding year. Additional measurement categories, such as quality, were added; budget processes were refined and streamlined; new systems were installed or integrated; executive information systems and relational data bases were tested; standard cost systems were installed; and targets were adjusted. Throughout the period, all four managers used newly created diagnostic control systems to demonstrate their progress in achieving critical performance variable goals.

Thus, the four levers of control were effective in helping managers deal with such major challenges as overcoming organizational inertia, structuring and communicating performance expectations, and gaining organizational allegiance to the new agenda. Longer term, these systems focused attention on strategic uncertainties and enabled the emergence of new strategic initiatives.

Cluster 2: Strategic Evolution

"If you are coming in on the heels of success, it's harder to get change. You have to let them know you admire and appreciate the past success and that you understand the elements of that success. But you have to set up processes so that they can conclude that the changes you want are necessary."
William D. Ruckelshaus (1992), CEO, Browning-Ferris Industries

In contrast to the four managers attempting strategic turnaround, six managers in the study were taking over successful businesses. Four were replacing retiring CEOs; one was filling a vacancy created by the accidental death of the CEO; and one was brought in as part of an acquisition by a new parent company. These managers were not given an explicit mandate for change; their mandate was to continue a trajectory of profitable growth.

In some ways, these managers faced a more daunting task than the other four managers. Because their predecessors were perceived as successful, these newly appointed managers could not publicly criticize them or their strategies. Thus, there was no dramatic way to create a rallying call for change. Yet, each manager recognized that change and strategic renewal were necessary if the business was to continue its profitable growth in the face of rapidly changing product markets.

All six managers intended to continue the basic trajectory of the business but to shift the strategy to a direction they considered essential for successful competition in the decade ahead. Like the four managers engineering revolutionary change, four of the six managers conducted in-depth economic analyses during the first three months of their tenure to help them understand the strengths and weaknesses of the business. Three of the six hired strategy consulting firms to undertake specific analyses and projects.

For this group of managers, personal background was important in defining the themes of strategic renewal. Three had been promoted from within the organization and three had been recruited externally. The can manufacturer, whose previous experience had been in procurement, wished to refocus the supply side of the business through long-term, upstream contracts and market alliances. The president of the branded consumer product company, whose background included a term as president of an international subsidiary, wanted to roll out domestic product lines to international markets and to introduce more emphasis on technology. The paper company manager, who had been the CEO of a small, well-respected niche paper company, wished to inject more customer focus and marketing emphasis in his new company. The machinery manufacturer, who had risen in a high technology part of the business, planned to introduce more research and development focus to augment technology-based products. The electric utility president wanted conservation and environmental concerns to be the cornerstone of the organization's new strategy. The retail merchant expressed desire to create synergy among its three disparate divisions.

For the first twelve months of their tenures, these managers perceived three urgent demands:

- forcing the organization to feel uneasy with current performance
- teaching the organization the agenda for strategic renewal
- testing to ensure that agendas were being altered to allow the implementation of new strategic directions

The use of formal control systems played a role in meeting all three of these demands.

Using Management Control Systems to Generate Uneasiness with Current Performance

"I am introducing a new common language focusing on (1) earnings growth, (2) cash flow, and (3) return-on-capital-employed. I am setting targets at 19% return-on-

capital-employed and 9% growth in our asset base. If a business cannot meet these returns, I will be asking why we should be funding that business."

Each of these six managers began his tenure by communicating his agenda for strategic renewal through speeches, newsletters, and audiovisual materials. As new strategic themes were articulated to the organization, each manager established new financial control targets at more demanding levels.

Targets focused on such accounting variables as profitability, asset utilization, revenue or earnings growth, and working capital. While the accounting-based targets did not relate directly to the strategy of the business, targets were set at demanding levels and represented a significant increase in performance levels compared to previous periods. This action dramatically increased performance expectations, thereby confronting complacency and creating a sense of urgency.

Each of the six managers reinforced a sense of urgency through the use of incentive compensation. Incentive compensation was adjusted to focus attention on diagnostic control systems targets, and pay outs were based on formulas tied to the performance measured by control systems. Achievement, not effort, determined bonuses. New quantitative targets in each firm were related to accounting measures such as return on capital employed, asset growth, revenue growth, and operating profit. In one firm in which bonuses had been awarded on the basis of the manager's subjective evaluation of performance, the new manager changed the formula in such a way that 75 percent of the bonus was based on achieving quantitative targets and only 25 percent was based on the achievement of personal goals. The short-term, qualitative component of incentive compensation was linked to individual objectives that supported new strategic initiatives, for example, arranging new contracts, introducing technology, entering new markets.

In two of the six firms incentive formulas explicitly calibrated performance against industry competitors. In one firm, no bonuses were paid unless the firm's return on equity ranked in the top half of the industry; in the second firm, performance targets were established by reference to industry leaders. In all six firms, bonus formulas were altered to introduce a longer time horizon. Pay outs were based on financial performance not only in the current year but also over a longer time period (typically three years). One firm, for example, instituted a formula based on return on capital employed and asset growth using a three-year moving average to assign bonuses to its top 100 managers.

Like the managers in Cluster 1, these six managers placed great importance in having adequate diagnostic control systems to monitor performance targets. Four of the six firms already had strong diagnostic control systems in place, so no further investment in systems was necessary. In the two remaining firms, however, diagnostic control systems were not adequate. In one of these firms, the manager hired a new chief financial officer, who was given the assignment of installing new financial measurement systems. In the other firm, the manager hired consultants to install new financial systems.

These changes not only heightened expectations but also forced participants to think about the programs and strategies that could achieve the expected results. Participants throughout the organization realized that status quo behavior would not produce the improvements in financial performance that were needed for bonus incentives.

Using Management Control Systems to Teach the New Agenda for Strategic Renewal

"The business was superbly run tactically, but I didn't like their strategy. So I brought them here for a week to talk about strategy. We came out with a list of eight strategic priorities. One of the priorities was to throw away the existing business plan and deliver a new one to me in sixty days."

Educating the organization about the strategic agendas that will be encouraged and supported is a major challenge for managers engineering strategic renewal. This education was done both formally and informally by the six new managers. Informally, new strategic initiatives were a constant source of discussion. More formally, each manager issued formal planning guidelines that conveyed strategic agendas.

With one exception, these businesses had basic diagnostic planning systems, such as business planning and profit planning, in place. Each manager, however, changed or augmented planning to introduce greater importance and formality to the process. Typical changes included introducing new planning processes (e.g., capital budgeting; strategic planning; technology planning); lengthening planning horizons to encompass additional planning years; and increased emphasis on overall product market strategies and reduced emphasis on financial detail. In the business that was the exception, the manager brought in consultants to design and implement basic systems.

Each manager used the revised planning process to teach the organization the agenda for strategic renewal. Planning guidelines required subordinates to respond directly to the manager with action plans relating to the new strategic themes. The manager in one firm, for example, requested a "road map" from subordinates that would detail how they would inject new technology in their businesses over the next five years. Other managers asked subordinates to explain in specific detail how they would support the strategic agendas that were to be implemented.

Using Management Control Systems to Test the Organization

One change I am making is requiring managers to prepare a preliminary plan due by the first of October here at corporate. Last year, I asked people to develop highly detailed plans and they spent a lot of time doing analysis and preparing numbers and then, when they presented the plan to me, I realized that it was completely inadequate and threw the whole thing out. This ended up being terribly demoralizing. This year we are asking them to prepare a preliminary plan that states the direction they intend to take. The key is to test the strategy, the learning that is required in the business, and the estimated financials. This step allows me to take someone aside on an individual basis if their plan is way off the mark and it gives the two of us time to discuss what needs to be done to change the plan and make it more acceptable to me.

During early attempts to respond to the annual planning cycle, many of the plans submitted by subordinates were discarded as inadequate or pushed back for significant reworking. In these cases, subordinates had failed to identify new strategic initiatives that responded to the manager's agenda of strategic renewal. Diagnostic control processes were subsequently changed in each of the six firms to allow managers to test subordinates to determine if the themes of strategic renewal were incorporated in their implementation plans. These review sessions could be traumatic for the subordinates involved—one manager described the sessions as "sweating exercises." Testing acted as a catalyst for additional teaching and involved a high degree of learning, both about the desired substance of the plans and about how to manage the process. Failures to create strategic agendas to the satisfaction of these six managers resulted in one-on-one teaching/ testing sessions in which managers explained repeatedly why plans were inadequate and what additional initiatives were required. Managers also used this process to determine which subordinates were capable of the type of strategic change the managers valued.

"I sketched out the strategic plan for the business after I realized that if I asked them for it, all I would get would be a lot of numbers. I wrote it, gave it to them, and they re-wrote it and gave it back to me. So I re-wrote it again. We went back and forth four times. We spent three months agreeing on a plan that reflected what we are trying to achieve. We went through some hell to get it right, but we finally arrived at an eight page document that I was happy with."

By the second annual planning cycle, both process and content had improved. The new managers changed the process to request brief preliminary plans in advance of detailed plans. This step allowed more efficient testing of the general direction proposed by subordinates. The content of plans also improved as the organization learned what types of initiatives supported the new agenda. Thus, by the second planning cycle, subordinates passed the test more easily.

Intensive goal setting exercises can result in extreme pressure to meet performance expectations, especially when subordinates know that managers are evaluating their potential and bonuses are linked by formula to results. During the period under study, subordinates in two of the six businesses were discovered manipulating financial data to improve reported operating performance. In one company, this practice was particularly harmful because inventory and markdown decisions were then based on inaccurate data. In each case, the managers involved were fired, and new boundary systems were imposed immediately. In one firm, new policies were issued ("Investigation of Fraudulent or Wrongful Acts by an Employee"), a new position, Ombudsman, was created, and new reporting requirements were imposed on divisional controllers. In the other company, new procedures were implemented, audit staff was augmented, and reporting relationships were changed. As one manager observed, "Some things you never tolerate. The ends don't justify the means."

Using Management Control Systems to Focus Attention on Strategic Uncertainties

"I look at comparative sales daily for our retailing business and weekly for the others. In retailing, you can lose a million dollars in just one day. I use 'comp sales' as a gauge to what is happening in each of our businesses. It gives me a very quick way to know if business is up or down. More importantly, that information serves as a

catalyst throughout the organization to get people out in the field to find out what's going on."

The challenges facing each manager in Cluster 2 changed during the second twelve months of the study. Expectations had been raised, and the organization was beginning to comprehend the necessity of incorporating themes of strategic renewal into action plans. The concerns during the second twelve months of strategic renewal became similar to those of managers attempting more revolutionary change. As a result, each manager began devoting personal attention to an interactive control system that would focus organizational learning on the strategic uncertainties related to the new strategic agenda. New strategies emerged from the process. Two managers focused on strategic uncertainties related to the development and protection of new products and markets. These managers used profit planning systems interactively. One manager worried about fundamental changes in product technology that could erode the firm's ability to deliver low-cost products; another focused on leveraging proprietary technology to enter new markets. Both managers focused on project management systems that analyzed current and potential technical product attributes. The utility manager operated in a quasi-regulated market environment and therefore intensively monitored changes in the social and political environments through an interactive intelligence system. The fifth manager focused his attention on an interactive brand revenue budgeting system that supplied daily and weekly sales and volume statistics. This system focused learning on the impact of price, promotion, and packaging on customer buying patterns.

Relative Success

To what extent were the actions of these ten managers appropriate and therefore visible in improved performance? Although there should be a relationship between the management process variables of this study and business performance, intervening organizational and environmental variables make the measurement of performance relationships extremely difficult. The process choices are subtle, and the substance of the strategy chosen by managers and the past resource commitments of the firm are important determinants of success (Porter 1980, 1985; Ghemawat 1991).

Although economic performance effects cannot be calibrated easily, other dimensions of managerial effectiveness can be examined.

There were no obvious differences in effectiveness among the managers in Cluster 2. Over the eighteen months of this study, all appeared to be gaining support and implementing desired changes. There was, however, some variation in the perceived success of the managers in Cluster 1. All ten managers had visions of strategic change or renewal. Yet, support for change can be obtained only if managers signal their commitment to change through periodic, personal involvement in beliefs systems, boundary systems, diagnostic control systems, and interactive control systems. With two exceptions, managers in both clusters seemed able to allocate sufficient attention to these processes to signal their commitment.

In the second twelve months of their tenures, two managers—both in Cluster 1 where attention demands were most acute—were perceived by some subordinates as insufficiently attentive to key processes. As a result, there was a gradual reduction in organizational commitment to the strategic changes advocated by these two managers. Perhaps by coincidence, one of these managers resigned shortly after the completion of the study to become chief executive of another firm; the other was promoted to the nonoperating post of chairman to make way for a new, younger chief executive. The renewal attempts of these two managers cannot be deemed failures, however, because each of their successors continued the basic strategy they had set for the business.

By the end of the study, all ten managers were still in place and leading their businesses. One year after the completion of the study, however, only seven of the managers were still in position. In addition to the two managers mentioned above, a third manager was displaced by a merger and transferred to take on new responsibilities at another business within the same corporation.

Analysis of the Managers' Actions

"I have become an expert in the power of formal process and systems driving behavior. I believe that the finest managers are incredibly sensitive to these processes and their power."

As all ten managers in the sample were accomplished senior executives who had been hired or promoted on the basis of their proven track records, the consistency in the way they used management control systems may not be surprising. Exhibit 6.5 presents a summary of the actions undertaken by all the managers. Regardless of their mandate, newly appointed managers in both clusters used control systems to overcome organizational inertia; communicate the substance of their new agenda; structure implementation timetables and targets; ensure continuing attention through incentives; and focus organizational learning on the strategic uncertainties associated with their vision for the future.

These actions were instrumental in framing strategic domains, implementing desired strategies, and guiding the emergence of new strategic initiatives. In Gabarro's study of fourteen new profit center managers, the extent to which new managers made changes to information and control systems in their first year emerged as one of the strongest findings:

When a new manager's initial assessment showed that an existing system was inadequate in yielding the information needed to assess performance or diagnose problems, he typically responded by initiating changes in the system (or in some cases by implementing a new system) that would provide information. *Systems changes were made in all but one of the longitudinal cases during the first three to six months.* (Gabarro 1987, 77, emphasis added)

The data reported in this chapter confirm the importance of formal management systems as levers of change and suggest that managers use these levers consistently and actively to control business strategy.

Managers in both clusters perceived a need to break old behavioral patterns and upset organizational inertia.[3] Managers with a mandate for revolutionary change could declare the past strategies failures and use strategic boundaries and new formal beliefs systems to set a new course. Managers taking over successful businesses, however, could not criticize past strategies to create a catalyst for change. Instead, they had to rely on demanding financial targets, administered through diagnostic control systems, to create a sense of urgency and awareness that old behaviors would no longer suffice.

Similarly, managers in both clusters altered incentives but did so in different ways. The managers in Cluster 1 made bonus incentives largely subjective during the first year in an attempt to capture allegiance to the new strategy. The managers who were attempting evolutionary change linked bonuses to financial results by formulas.

---

[3] For a discussion of this phenomenon in another setting, see Pettigrew (1985), pp. 462–63.

Purpose	Cluster 1: Strategic Turnaround Mandate	Cluster 2: Strategic Evolution Mandate
First twelve months:		
1. Overcome organizational inertia →	Formalize and communicate strategic boundaries	Use diagnostic controls to: • Link bonuses to financial targets • Raise minimum performance levels for financial targets
2. Communicate substance of new agenda →	Formalize new strategy and communicate through new mission statements (beliefs systems) Use diagnostic control systems in presentations to superiors	Issue planning guidelines to subordinates outlining new strategic initiatives
3. Establish implementation timetable and targets →	Based on commitments made to superiors, fix accountability targets with subordinates Link diagnostic control system targets to critical performance variables	Use diagnostic control systems to teach and test new agenda Link diagnostic control system targets to critical performance variables
4. Ensure continuing attention through incentives →	Alter bonus incentives to be subjectively determined based on allegiance to new strategic agenda	Alter bonus incentives to be formula based and linked to new, more demanding financial targets Institute business conduct boundaries in response to control system manipulation
Second twelve months:		
5. Focus organization learning on strategic uncertainties associated vision for the future	Begin using one control system interactively to signal priorities and motivate debate and dialogue	Begin using one control system interactively to signal priorities and motivate debate and dialogue

Exhibit 6.5 Summary of Control Lever Usage by Newly Appointed Top Managers

Subordinates were forced to rethink how these demanding financial targets could be achieved. This finding highlights the power of incentives in focusing attention. I have argued in Chapter 5 that subjective incentives are used to calibrate contribution with interactive control systems; managers also seem to use subjective incentives when allegiance to a new management team is essential. As discussed in Chapter 4, formula-based incentives are used to build "stretch" targets necessary to influence behavior patterns.

Planning systems—the diagnostic control systems used to implement strategy—were important elements of communicating and implementing agendas. In Cluster 2, managers used these systems to teach and test the new agenda. Other studies have recognized that managers wishing to change the direction of an organization can use goals to create challenges and break existing patterns of action (Quinn 1977). Some authors have likened the business leader to a teacher, but they have tended to focus exclusively on the teacher as facilitator and coach (Senge 1990). The important role of testing and accountability has often been neglected.

In both clusters, the use of management control systems progressed through distinct stages that can be associated with systematic attempts to foster both learning and unlearning. In Cluster 1, boundary systems promoted the unlearning of old behavior patterns, a necessary condition for change. Beliefs systems were used to provide a new frame of reference for the changes to follow. Changes in diagnostic control systems focused organizational attention on the critical performance variables that would support the implementation of the new strategy. Finally, the introduction of interactive systems put in place a formal way of generating dialogue, debate, and learning that allowed new strategic initiatives to emerge.

Management control systems also appear to be vitally important in building credibility and selling a new strategy to various constituents. To implement strategy effectively, Hambrick and Cannella have argued that managers must "sell, sell, sell the strategy to everyone who matters—upward, downward, across, and outward" (1989, 278). New managers in both clusters were consistent in the way they used management control system targets to communicate direction and create credibility with both superiors and subordinates.

Summary

Management control systems are critical levers for strategic change and renewal. They are put in place to respond to information and control needs as organizations grow, but these levers are neither static nor deterministic. They can be used in many ways to suit the agendas of individual managers in different strategic contexts.

This chapter has provided a glimpse of the processes used by senior managers in controlling organizations and implementing business strategies. Some techniques are subtle; some less so. All are important in conserving scarce attention and focusing opportunity-seeking behavior.

CHAPTER 7

The Dynamics of Controlling Strategy

Previous chapters have laid out basic assumptions, described the control levers, and illustrated how top managers use these levers to drive change. Each control lever was differentiated as much as possible to highlight its unique characteristics and attributes. Now that we have considered each separately, an important proposition can be stated: Control of business strategy is achieved by integrating the forces of beliefs systems, boundary systems, diagnostic control systems, and interactive control systems. The power of the control levers does not lie in how each is used alone but rather in how they complement each other when used together. The interplay of positive and negative forces generated by these systems creates a dynamic tension between the opportunistic innovation and predictable goal achievement that is necessary for profitable growth.

The four levers can now be integrated into a framework that recognizes the major tensions discussed in Chapter 2: (1) unlimited opportunity versus limited attention, (2) intended versus emergent strategy, and (3) self-interest versus the desire to contribute.

Using the Control Levers to Guide Strategy

Before focusing on the dynamics of these systems, we must revisit the nature of the strategy process. As discussed in Chapter 1,

153

Opportunity Space

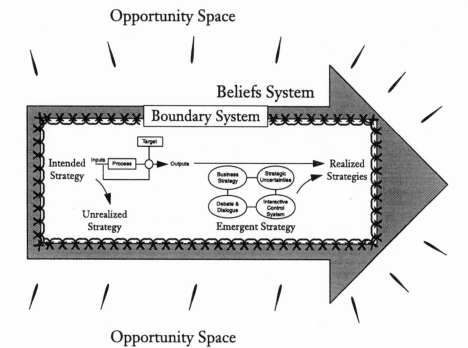

Opportunity Space

Figure 7.1   Relationship Between Levers of Control and Realized Strategies

strategy can be described as a plan, a pattern of actions, a product-market position, or a unique perspective. Moreover, any theory of control must be sensitive to the distinction between intended and emergent strategy. The challenge is to develop theories of control that recognize the roles of these various types of strategy.

To aid in the analysis, consider briefly the distinction among intended strategies, emergent strategies, and realized strategies (Mintzberg 1978). This distinction will prove to be important in understanding how formal systems control business strategy (Figure 7.1).

Realized strategies are a combination of intended and emergent strategies that are successful. Realized strategies are outcomes that are evident to observers of the firm, such as the businesss press, and to those who interact with it, such as customers and competitors.

As noted in Chapter 3, diagnostic control systems coordinate and monitor the implementation of intended strategies. The targets and goals embedded in formal plans are the embodiment of management's intended strategies. Diagnostic control systems, then, relate to strategy as a plan. These systems are essential management tools for transforming intended strategies into realized strategies because they focus attention on goal achievement for the business and the individual. At the business level, the strategy of any firm is the aggregation of strategies that affect financing, marketing, production, distribution, government relations, and so forth. Diagnostic control systems are designed to gain coherence over the multiple functional strategies that coalesce into realized strategies. At the individual level, diagnostic control systems provide the focus, resources, and goals that allow individuals to satisfy innate desires for achievement and recognition.

Some intended strategies, however, may go unrealized: goals may be set inappropriately or circumstances may change, making goal achievement either impossible or less desirable. Some intended strategies are never implemented because unanticipated roadblocks are encountered or resources are insufficient. Managers in large organizations can ascertain if intended strategies are realized only if those strategies are monitored by a diagnostic control system, which allows them to measure outcomes and compare results with *a priori* plans and goals.

Interactive control systems give managers tools to influence the experimentation and opportunity-seeking that may result in emergent strategies. Thus interactive control systems facilitate and shape the emergence of new strategies. These systems relate to *strategy as patterns of action*. At the business level, even in the absence of formal plans and goals, managers who use these systems are able to impose consistency and guide creative search processes. Tactical day-to-day actions and creative experiments can be welded into a cohesive pattern that responds to strategic uncertainties and may, over time, become realized strategy.

At the individual level, interactive control systems help to satisfy innate desires to create and innovate. These systems facilitate, encourage, and provide opportunity for experimentation and reward creative thinking.

The beliefs system of the organization inspires both intended and emergent strategies. Management's vision, expressed in mission statements and related systems, motivates organizational participants to search for and create opportunities to accomplish the overall mission of the firm. Beliefs systems appeal to the innate desires of organizational participants to belong and contribute to purposive organizations. These systems relate to strategy as perspective. The beliefs system creates direction and momentum to fuse intended and emergent strategies together and provides guidance and inspiration for individual opportunity-seeking.

In many ways, the most difficult part of strategic analysis lies in determining what you do *not* want to do and where you do *not* want to compete. Boundary systems ensure that realized strategies fall within the acceptable domain of activities. Boundary systems control strategy as "position," ensuring that business activities occur in defined product markets and at acceptable levels of risk. Without boundary systems, which reduce opportunity space and focus opportunity-seeking behavior by delimiting core ethical, strategic, and operating boundaries, creative opportunity-seeking behavior and experimentation can dissipate the resources of the firm. Boundary systems make explicit the costs that will be imposed on participants who wander outside the boundaries to engage in proscribed behaviors. Exhibit 7.1 summarizes the relationship between the four central levers and strategy.

Strategic control is not achieved through new and unique systems but through beliefs systems, boundary systems, diagnostic control systems, and interactive control systems working in concert to control both the implementation of intended strategies and the formation of emergent strategies. These systems provide the motivation, measurement, learning, and control that allow efficient goal achievement, creative adaptation, and profitable growth. Each of these sys-

Control System	Purpose	Communicates	Control of Strategy as
Beliefs Systems	Empower and expand search activity	Vision	Perspective
Boundary Systems	Provide limits of freedom	Strategic domain	Competitive position
Diagnostic Control Systems	Coordinate and monitor the implementation of intended strategies	Plans and goals	Plan
Interactive Control Systems	Stimulate and guide emergent strategies	Strategic uncertainties	Pattern of actions

Exhibit 7.1   Relating the Four Control Levers to Strategy

Opportunity and Attention

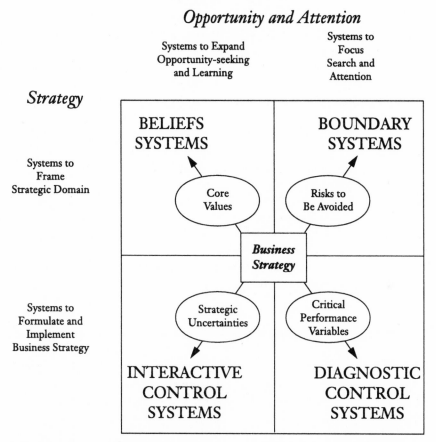

Figure 7.2 Interrelation of the Levers of Control with Strategy, Opportunity, and Attention

tems, as shown in Figure 7.2, has a different purpose in controlling strategy.

Beliefs systems empower and expand opportunity seeking. Boundary systems set the rules of competition. Together, beliefs systems and boundary systems frame the strategic domain for the organization. Diagnostic control systems focus attention on the implementation of intended strategies. Finally, interactive control systems expand and guide the opportunity-seeking that may result in the emergence of strategies. Together, diagnostic control systems and interactive control systems guide the implementation and formulation of strategy.

As noted earlier, the four systems are nested: each offers some measure of guidance or control to the strategy process, but each system is *used* in different ways for different purposes. These different usage patterns are critical in leveraging scarce management attention to maximize return-on-management (ROM). Interactive control requires ongoing and intensive managerial involvement; diagnostic controls need periodic and exception-based involvement; and beliefs and boundary systems require only sufficient downward communication to ensure that core values and rules of the game are understood. Diagnostic control systems conserve management attention; interactive systems amplify management attention. Staff groups play an important role in maximizing ROM by complementing the amount of attention, or, more important, inattention, that managers devote to each system: staff groups act as media consultants and messengers for beliefs systems; as facilitators for interactive control systems; as technical experts, gatekeepers, and emissaries for diagnostic control systems; and as policemen for boundary systems.

Dynamic Interplay of Forces

The dynamic energy for controlling strategy derives from inherent tensions among and within these systems (Figure 7.3). Two of the control systems motivate organizational participants to search creatively and expand opportunity space. These are the positive systems—the yang of Chinese philosophy. The other two systems are used to constrain search behavior and allocate scarce attention. These are the negative systems—the opposing yin. Beliefs systems and interactive control systems create intrinsic motivation in organizational participants by creating a positive informational environment that encourages information sharing and learning (Deci and Ryan 1985, 96). Boundary systems and diagnostic control systems create extrinsic motivation by providing formula-based rewards and delimiting the domain for opportunity-seeking.

Control is achieved when the tension between creative innovation and predictable goal achievement is transformed into profitable growth. This tension implies that effective organizations must achieve simultaneously high degrees of learning and high degrees of control. This proposition parallels the arguments of Lawrence and Dyer who found that organizational adaptation requires high levels of both efficiency and innovation:

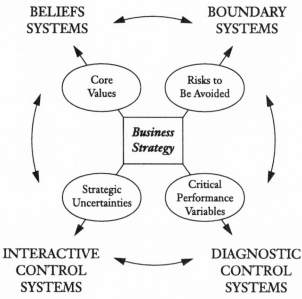

Figure 7.3 A Dynamic Relationship

In industry after industry, competitors around the world are proving that organizations must be *both* efficient and innovative if they are to remain on the leading edge. . . . Efficiency and innovation are difficult to reconcile. In the short run, these two performance targets can impede and block each other; innovations coming from the development laboratory are a hindrance to maintaining current production efficiency, while a drive, for instance, to cut costs in the name of efficiency is almost certain to reduce the budget for innovation. This tension is often expressed as a struggle between short-term and long-term policy, between the necessary looseness of creativity and the necessary rigidity of control. *The process by which organizations repeatedly recon-*

cile efficiency and innovation is called the readaptive process. . . . For the readaptive process to be sustained, organizational members need to learn *in order to be innovative and need to* strive *in order to be efficient. . . .*

Certain internal conditions must be met if the total membership of an organization is to be involved in the learning and striving necessary for the readaptive process. In the first place, the organization must clearly and systematically communicate to the membership its goals and expectations. There must be as little ambiguity as possible regarding the principles underlying the organizational strategy, structure, and practices. Briefly, *the readaptive process depends on an organization's entire membership being made cognizant of the broad purpose, ethical standards, and operating principles of the firm with emphasis given throughout to the value of both efficiency and innovation.* (1983, 8–10, italics in original)

The formal systems enumerated in this analysis are capable of reconciling the tensions between innovation and efficiency. All four control systems have elements of both control and learning, and all four work simultaneously. Boundary systems are weighted heavily to control and limits. However, they also reflect learning since past mistakes and the tactical moves of competitors dictate the adjustment of ethical and strategic boundaries. Diagnostic control systems clearly emphasize control and efficiency, but setting goals, measuring outcomes, remedying variances, and assigning rewards involve elements of innovation and learning. It is mostly single-loop learning, but, occasionally, double-loop learning occurs (Argyris and Schön 1978, 18–20). Interactive control systems also involve both control and learning although learning and innovation dominate as senior managers use the interactive control process as a catalyst to force the organization to monitor changing market dynamics and motivate debate about data, assumptions, and action plans. Over time, the information and learning generated by interactive control systems can be embedded in the strategies and goals that are monitored by diagnostic control systems.

Not only is there an interplay of motivational forces among the four systems, there is also a tension of motivational forces within each system. Boundary systems, for example, are powered by both direct threats of punishment and innate desires to do right. Diagnostic systems are motivated by wealth-enhancing economic rewards and innate desires to achieve and be recognized by others. Interactive systems are powered by the personal intervention of senior managers as well as participants' innate desires to innovate and create.

For any organizational participant at any point in time, countervailing forces are at work. These four systems, then, are mutually reinforcing. The creative tensions between learning and control, between guidance and proscription, between motivation and coercion, between rewards and punishment become the yin and yang—dynamic forces that simultaneously foster both stability and change. Collectively, these forces control both the human traits and organizational blocks discussed in Chapter 2.

As the pace and experience of organizational life unfolds, these forces are constantly in flux. Beliefs are reinforced and recommunicated by senior managers on an irregular basis; annual planning processes redefine strategic boundaries in unexpected ways; regular discussions triggered by an interactive control system create new agendas and action plans; new measures and bonus schemes are devised to monitor the implementation of changing goals and strategies.

Tight Versus Loose Control

The concept of tight versus loose control has troubled theorists for many years. Tight control implies severe limits to an individual's degrees of freedom, thereby assuring that he or she will behave as the organization wishes (Merchant 1985, ch. 6). Loose control implies that individuals have a great deal of autonomy and freedom. Management theorists have generally treated "tightness of controls" as a unitary concept that can be tilted toward either tighter or looser controls.

Faced with evidence that organizations use tight and loose controls simultaneously, however, popular management writing has suggested that managers should employ controls with "simultaneous loose-tight" properties (Peters and Waterman 1982, ch. 12). Such suggestions underscore a lack of understanding about the nature of control processes in complex organizations.

The framework developed here suggests that the concept of "tightness of controls" is of little value unless it is differentiated according to the multiple types of control levers and how they are used. In any organization, at any point in time, and at any level, managers will report varying degrees of "tightness" in respect of beliefs systems, boundary systems, diagnostic control systems, and interactive control systems. For example, Jane Smith, a senior manager, may feel that her budget targets are difficult, inflexible, and subject to careful monitoring by staff specialists. These diagnostic controls are tight, but superiors exhibit only periodic interest unless important targets are missed.

At the same time, the project management system used in the business is highly interactive. As a result, Smith interacts almost daily with superiors, peers, and subordinates in an attempt to provide, understand, and challenge information in the system and act upon that information. Scrutiny of her thinking and action proposals are intense as senior managers and Smith's immediate superior meet frequently to discuss the information generated by the system, to generate proposals and action plans, and to test new ideas. But Jane Smith feels relatively unconstrained in the way the task is approached and knows that targets can be adjusted if necessary based on updated information.

Finally, Smith has clearly delineated boundary systems that tell her the standards of conduct expected of her and the product markets in which she *cannot* look for opportunity. Because so much opportunity remains in the areas where she can search, however, she feels only the loosest of constraints affecting her search behavior.

To understand how well-managed companies build simultaneous "loose-tight" properties into their control systems, observers must understand the nature and effects of the four control levers to predict when, how, and why a senior manager might use any given control system and the effect of that choice on organizational behavior.

Balancing Empowerment and Control

Running through this book is the theme of organizational tension: unlimited opportunity versus limited attention; top-down versus bottom-up strategy; innovation versus predictability; learning versus control. The current trend to "empower" participants of business organizations has created another set of tensions.

As markets have become increasingly competitive and fast moving, managers have realized they must push decision making down to employees who are in close contact with customers. Empowering employees—moving decision-making authority from higher to lower levels in the organization—is a necessary condition for building responsive organizations. At the same time, however, the ceding of decision authority to subordinates can be dangerous. One large pharmaceutical company that faced increasing cost competition encouraged its mid-level managers to become more responsive to customers

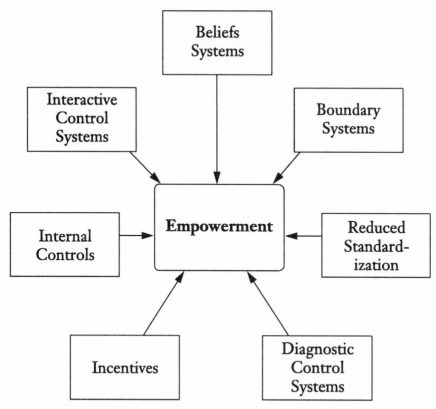

Figure 7.4 Balancing Empowerment and Control

when drawing up new equipment contracts with hospitals. Some sales managers began to provide hospitals with expensive diagnostic machines at no charge (thereby responding to the hospital's desire to conserve scarce capital appropriations) with the arrangement that disposable reagent supplies for the machine would be purchased later at above market prices. Before long, managers began to rewrite contract terms to reflect these arrangements without sufficient regard for the enforceability and collectability of the contracts. The result was a multi-million dollar write-off of contract receivables.

Most writing on empowerment fails to recognize that empowerment requires greater control. The control systems used, however, must balance empowerment and control in such a way that empowerment does not lead to a control failure, and correspondingly, control does not lead to an empowerment failure. Figure 7.4 illustrates the controls that create an empowered, market-driven organization.

Effective empowerment does not just push decision-making and resources down several levels in the organization. To unleash their potential to innovate and make local decisions more effectively, subordinates must have information and training: information to provide awareness of potential problems, opportunities, and available resources; training to use the tools they need to act effectively to meet local needs. Even with information and training, however, employees cannot be effectively empowered without the following controls in place.

Beliefs Systems. As a backdrop to empowered decision making, organizational participants must clearly understand the basic purpose, values, and direction of the organization. In attempting to respond to market threats and opportunities, employees can undertake a wide array of actions, and senior managers cannot predict the novel solutions they may devise. Clear principles and values as well as a clear understanding of the business mission are necessary to guide organizational participants to make appropriate trade-offs.

Boundary Systems. Notwithstanding the delegation of decision rights and the effective communication of core values and beliefs, opportunistic search behavior cannot be unbounded. Empowerment does not mean that organizational participants can do whatever they please. There must be guidelines that clearly state the types of behavior that are prohibited. These guidelines must come from senior managers who must define the types of behaviors that are potentially damaging to the organization and prohibit employees from undertaking these actions.

Reduced Standardization. Organizations that control inputs and production (or service) processes through detailed standard operating procedures cannot empower organizational participants to respond creatively to customer needs or to devise improved ways of operating the business. To empower their participants, these organizations must review long-standing practices and tasks to ensure that excessive standardization is not limiting opportunities for creativity. Work standards, formalized guidelines, and policy manuals must be reduced drastically, especially for any activity deemed to be a critical performance variable in the implementation of strategy. Terms such as "workouts" and "process reengineering" are popular labels that are

Standardization

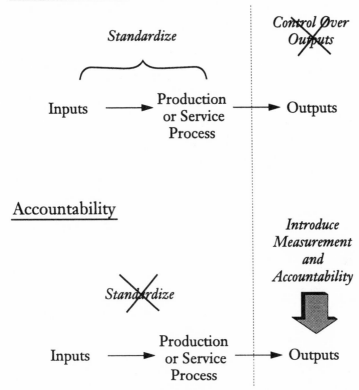

Figure 7.5   Alternative Approaches to Control

used to describe attempts to eliminate inappropriate levels of standardization.

Diagnostic Control Systems. Empowerment does not mean giving up control, but it does change what is controlled. In the absence of control over inputs or process, individuals must be held accountable for their outputs or performance. A subordinate cannot be empowered if he or she cannot be held accountable for performance. Diagnostic control systems capable of measuring results become critically important. These systems leave it up to employees to figure out how to juggle inputs and processes to achieve the output the systems require (Figure 7.5).

Although performance measures must be tailored to the tasks

of individuals throughout the organization, they create performance pressures that can stimulate innovation. In addition, these systems allow managers to assess the extent to which intended strategies are being realized.

Incentives. In an empowered organization, individuals are asked to assume more responsibility and, therefore, they assume more risks. Thus, there must be incentives to take risks, and rewards for superior performance. Rewards must reflect this new responsibility and honor those who rise to the challenge. Rewards can be either economic or noneconomic (public recognition and prestige), but should be presented on the basis of an individual's contribution to the mission of the business.

Internal Controls. Internal controls, which are usually accounting-based and managed by accountants and internal auditors, provide the procedural checks and balances that safeguard assets and assure integrity of data. While these controls are essential in any organization, they are especially critical in organizations that put performance pressure on individuals, introduce contribution-based rewards, and at the same time, reduce standardization and procedural controls for many of the critical aspects of their jobs. Without basic internal controls, the risks of significant control failure become unacceptably high.

Interactive Control Systems. Interactive control systems provide the formal information conduits to transmit learning up, down, and sideways in the organization and thus capture the benefits of employee initiative. A great deal of experimentation can occur within the area created by a set of guiding beliefs, reduction of standardizing work rules, strong performance expectations, and rewards for individual contributions. Interactive control systems help to focus attention on areas of strategic uncertainty and help participants to assimilate and share the learning that results from this focus.

Implications for Managers

Key Strategic Variables to be Analyzed

To implement strategy effectively, senior managers must have a clear understanding of four key strategic variables: core values; risks to

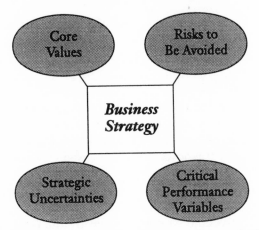

Figure 7.6 Controlling Business Strategy: Strategic Variables to Be Analyzed

be avoided; critical performance variables; and strategic uncertainties (Figure 7.6). These four variables are highly interdependent. For example, core values influence strategy and critical performance variables. Core values also define the levels of acceptable risk and strategic uncertainties. The same interrelatedness is found among the other three variables. Strategic uncertainties can only be understood against a backdrop of core values, risks to be avoided, and critical performance variables. For this reason, they must be analyzed together. Analysis of only one or two in isolation will yield an incomplete understanding of the issues that must be controlled to implement strategy effectively.

Core values. The core values of any organization are rooted in its *history, traditions*, and the *values* of its current senior managers. Core values create momentum that can either help or hinder the implementation of business strategies. These values are the starting point for determining the competencies of an organization.

Managers must analyze the core values of their business to understand the extent to which they are in tune with the desired strategic direction. For many years, IBM's core values related to the mastery of complex technologies and a marketing prowess that focused on large commercial customers. The strongly held and clearly articulated beliefs of its founder, Thomas J. Watson, created a sense of pride to IBM employees all over the world (Watson 1963, 1990). In the 1990s, as IBM struggles to redefine itself in changing markets, these same values are liabilities.

Beliefs systems help to reinforce or change values. Although they are only one lever in a complicated set of forces related to core values, they are one of the few levers that senior managers can use directly to inspire search for opportunity. However, unless managers understand the current core values of the organization, the values they wish to reinforce, and the relationship of these values to the business strategy of the firm, this lever cannot be used effectively.

Risks to be avoided. Every business faces risks that can damage the success of the enterprise. The nature of the industry in which a firm competes and the specific strategy chosen by the firm determine the risks to be avoided. Managers in the construction industry, for example, recognize that bribing public officials can subject a business to severe penalties and ruin its reputation. Large consulting firms that deal in highly sensitive data, such as Bain and McKinsey, risk damaging their reputations if proprietary data is leaked.

Effective managers understand that a critical part of strategic analysis is determining and communicating the risks to be avoided. Strategic risks to be avoided are determined by the desired direction of the firm and an assessment of core competencies. Managers of a telecommunications firm must decide whether to declare satellite design inside or outside the boundaries of permissible activity. A pharmaceutical company must decide which therapeutic classes it will not investigate. Squandering resources on multiple projects and initiatives that lack coherence is a recipe for failure.

Boundary systems cannot be designed without the explicit recognition of the risks that flow from both the dynamics of industry competition and strategic choices made by the firm. Implementing a strategy successfully requires the anticipation and proactive control of the risks associated with that strategy.

Critical performance variables. Critical performance variables are a function of the competitive strategies a firm chooses. A manager must understand the critical performance variables that define successful performance to set objectives and measure progress against stated strategic goals. The critical performance variables of a discount retailer differ from the critical performance variables of a retailer that competes on full price and service. A manager must ask repeatedly, "What are the critical factors that must be implemented successfully for the intended strategy to succeed? How do they affect cost, marketing, finance, human resources, technology?" As strategies change, so do critical performance variables. Consultants and staff specialists often have the necessary expertise to identify these strategic variables and design diagnostic control systems for them.

Strategic uncertainties. Strategic uncertainties are a joint function of senior management's vision for the future and their assessment of the contingencies that could undermine that vision. Senior managers should be able to articulate a vision of how the business will evolve over the next five to ten years and the key contingencies that could derail this vision. While senior managers at USA Today, for example, envision a color-format national newspaper that combines national advertising and copy with regionally tailored circulation, this vision depends on targeting the key industries that can mount national advertising campaigns. Senior management needs to monitor these contingencies carefully to ensure that their assumptions are still valid. Although interactive control systems can trigger organizational learning about strategic uncertainties and the evolution of new tactics and strategies, they cannot be effective unless managers can articulate their vision for the future and the related contingencies that could undermine that vision.

Achieving High Return-on-Management

An analysis of key strategic variables and a clear understanding of the four control levers is not sufficient to control the implementation of strategy. To maximize return-on-management, managers must understand how to leverage their limited time and attention. Staff groups complement the attention—or inattention—that top managers devote to different control systems. The tasks performed by managers and staff groups are outlined in Exhibit 7.2.

In using staff specialists to leverage scarce attention, however, caution is necessary. Sometimes control staff specialists attempt to impose an interactive control system on processes that should be controlled diagnostically. Staff experts find interactive control systems appealing because these systems receive management attention, thus they elevate the importance of staff work. Too often, staff experts create systems that will standardize and program tasks (thereby driving out creativity) and then set up procedures and schedules that will

	Managers	Staff Groups
Beliefs Systems	Personally prepare substantive drafts of beliefs statements Communicate message and importance	Facilitate awareness and communication through distribution of documents, education programs, and organizational surveys
Boundary Systems	Personally prepare strategic boundaries Review business conduct boundaries compiled by staff groups Mete out punishment personally to offenders	Prepare business conduct boundaries Communicate both strategic and business conduct boundaries Educate organization about important boundaries Monitor compliance
Diagnostic Control Systems	Periodically set or negotiate performance targets Receive and review exception reports Follow up significant exceptions	Design and maintain systems Interpret data Prepare exception reports Ensure integrity and reliability of data
Interactive Control Systems	Choose which system to use interactively Schedule frequent face-to-face meetings with subordinates to discuss data contained in system Demand that operating managers throughout the organization respond to information contained in the system	Gather and compile data Facilitate interactive process

Exhibit 7.2   Control System Tasks for Managers and Staff Groups

absorb senior management attention. Staff experts and management consultants who advocated strategic planning, zero-based budgeting, or management-by-objectives developed step-by-step procedures to program their favorite system and then attempted to schedule management meetings to create an interactive control system. If managers allow this error to persist, the systems will not yield the promised benefits and will tie up inappropriate amounts of management attention. To maximize ROM, senior managers must ensure that staff experts and operating managers throughout the organization are aware of their roles in each of the four levers of control.

Strategic planning programs and zero-based budgeting programs were discontinued or significantly reduced once managers understood that they were reducing innovation, inappropriately absorbing management attention, and driving down ROM. "Total quality" systems will probably share the same fate once managers understand the cost of control systems that attempt to program basic work processes and, at the same time, demand a great deal of attention from operating managers.

Realizing Human Potential

Effective managers must understand central tendencies to manage against them. Important assumptions underlie the analysis that is presented in this book, assumptions about how value is created, how strategies are formed, and how people behave in organizations. In the day-to-day life of organizations, these assumptions, which are unspoken and unchallenged, influence the ways in which managers control strategy and the extent to which their efforts are successful. These assumptions determine how managers deal with subordinates, how decision authority is delegated, and what types of behavior managers expect from themselves and the people who work for them.

Assumptions about human behavior entail real risks, risks that flow from the assumptions themselves and risks that the assumptions are wrong. This is the Type I and Type II error problem familiar to students of statistical inference. A Type I error occurs when we reject a hypothesis that is true; a Type II error occurs when we accept a hypothesis that is false.

Suppose that a manager must choose between two models of human behavior and treat subordinates accordingly. The first model postulates that subordinates are honest, hardworking, and fulfill their commitments to the best of their abilities. In this model, subordinates are potential to be unleashed. The second model views subordinates as inherently dishonest, lazy, and eager, if possible, to avoid fulfilling commitments that involve effort. In this model subordinates require careful monitoring and control.

If a manager chooses the first model and subordinates are honest and hard-working, the manager's efforts can be directed toward unleashing the potential of subordinates, who will respond to the opportunity that is provided to them to achieve and contribute.

The manager makes a Type I error if he or she chooses the second model and subordinates are actually hardworking and honest. In this case, subordinates will be denied the opportunity to participate in key decisions for fear that their self-interested behavior will be detrimental to the firm. As subordinates recognize the lack of trust, they will become unwilling to commit and work toward the goals of the organization. Gaming or other dysfunctional behavior may result. Thus, the Type I error becomes a self-fulfilling prophecy that blocks the contribution of subordinates and may lead to negative consequences for the firm.

On the other hand, if the manager accepts the first model when subordinates are lazy and adverse to effort, a Type II error has been committed. In this case, the actions of the manager will provide an opportunity for subordinates to shirk and misappropriate assets. The lack of necessary controls and monitoring will allow the self-interested behavior of subordinates to overtake organizational goals. A Type II error is costly to the firm.

These stylized examples are clearly overstated, but they illustrate the potential costs and pitfalls of incorrectly specifying human behavior. The assumptions a manager makes about human behavior are critical to the choices that must be made to control strategy.

Of course, there is evidence of both models in every organization. Humans value contribution and commitment but also exhibit traits of self-interest. In the absence of leadership and purpose, individuals will become self-interested and work for their own benefit with little regard to the goals of the organization. Effective controls must deal with both models. Nowhere is the tension between these two models more apparent than at business schools: the organizational behavior course emphasizes motivation through teamwork and commitment; the applied economics course focuses on compensation incentives as the primary driver of behavior.

The model of human behavior adopted in this book reconciles

Organization Man/Woman Desires to	Organizational Blocks	Managerial Solution	Relevant Control Lever
Contribute	Unsure of Purpose	Communicate core values and mission	Beliefs Systems
Do Right	Pressure or temptation	Specify and enforce rules of the game	Boundary Systems
Achieve	Lack of focus or resources	Build and support clear targets	Diagnostic Control Systems
Create	Lack of opportunity or afraid of risk	Open organizational dialogue to trigger learning	Interactive Control Systems

Exhibit 7.3   Human Behavior, Organizational Blocks, and the Levers of Control

these models by assuming that people desire (1) to achieve and contribute, (2) to do right, and (3) to create and innovate and that lapses in these behaviors are due to organizational blocks rather than to a misspecification of the nature of organizational work.

Exhibit 7.3 illustrates the links between these assumptions and managerial action. The first column specifies key behavioral assumptions; the second column lists the organizational blocks that often hinder human potential in organizations. The final two columns provide remedies—both in managerial actions and the use of the control levers.

Our model of human behavior assumes that people desire to contribute but that there can be organizational blocks to this behavior. Organizations often make it difficult for individuals to understand the larger purpose of their efforts or how they can add value in a way that matters. Effective managers recognize the organizational blocks and try to remove them by actively communicating core values and mission. In small organizations, this can and should be done informally whenever senior managers interact with subordinates. In larger organizations, managers must rely on formal systems (beliefs systems) to inspire organizational commitment and reduce organizational blocks.

Our model assumes that people desire to act in accordance with the moral codes of our society but that temptations and pressures always exist in organizations, which may lead to cutting corners, diverting assets, or otherwise choosing courses of action that are in conflict with stricter codes of behavior. Managers try to remove these blocks by clearly specifying and unambiguously enforcing the rules of the game. Some behaviors are never tolerated. The firing of the manager who inflated his or her expense report by $50 is a familiar story in many organizations. This action signals that the consequences of stepping over ethical boundaries, even in small ways, are severe and nonnegotiable. In larger organizations, managers must rely on formal boundary systems to ensure that these boundaries are communicated and understood.

Our model assumes that people desire to achieve, both for tangible rewards and because achievement can be an end in itself. Unfortunately, organizations can make achievement and the resulting sense of accomplishment difficult. Individuals may not be rewarded or recognized for their successes. Individuals may not be given the opportunity to focus their energies in ways that permit goals to be achieved and recognized. Often, resources are not available to allow people to rise to their potential. Effective managers attempt to remove these blocks by communicating clear targets and providing the necessary resources for achieving those targets. As organizations grow larger, managers use diagnostic controls to remove these blocks.

Finally, our model assumes that individuals want to innovate and create but that organizations often stifle this innate desire. Individuals either are denied the opportunity to experiment or fear the organizational risks that accompany challenges to the status quo. Effective managers remove these blocks by opening up channels for organizational dialogue and encouraging a learning environment that values dissent and new ideas. When organizations are small, this can be done informally. As organizations grow larger, interactive control systems are the catalyst for learning, experimentation, and information sharing.

Assumptions about human nature are at the core of using the levers of control effectively. Use Exhibit 7.3 to test your own assumptions of human behavior. Do you agree with the assumptions that underlie this theory? If not, what are your assumptions concerning human behavior? What are the implications of these behavioral assumptions for strategy formation and implementation? For empowerment? What are the effects of Type I and Type II errors if your assumptions are incorrect? Confronting and reconciling unstated assumptions of human behavior are the starting points for realizing human potential in organizations.

Summary

Effective top managers use the levers of control to inspire commitment to the organization's purpose; stake out the territory for experimentation and competition; coordinate and monitor the execution of today's strategies; and stimulate and guide the search for strategies of the future. Managing the tension between creative innovation and predictable goal achievement is the key to profitable growth.

In this book, I have attempted to demonstrate that management control systems are critical levers for the control of business strategy. These levers are used to balance organizational tensions. Tensions of control and learning, efficiency and innovation, reward and punishment, leadership and management are part of the fabric of organizations and sometimes make organizational life uncomfortable. As organizations grow, managers must deal with increasing opportunity, increasing competitive pressures, and decreasing time and attention. Finding ways to increase return-on-management becomes essential. The control levers are important tools in managing this balance; without these systems, modern organizations could not function.

Yet, these control levers represent very basic and simple processes: providing goals; telling people what they will be rewarded for; telling them what not to do; telling them what you believe in; asking for their ideas; sharing knowledge. These are basic human processes that are evident whenever people rely on leaders to direct collaborative enterprises toward worthwhile goals.

Appendix A
Checklist Summary of the Levers of Control

This Appendix presents four exhibits summarizing the "what," "why," "how," "when," and "who" of the four basic levers managers use to control the formation and implementation of business strategy: beliefs systems, boundary systems, diagnostic control systems, and interactive control systems.

Each summary provides a simplified checklist of the critical attributes for each control system and gives examples of its use.

The four levers differ both in technical design attributes and in managerial attention patterns (see Figure A.1, page 180). Beliefs systems and boundary systems differ from feedback and measurement systems in their technical design attributes—the type of information they contain, how information is disseminated, and the purpose of the system. Within measurement-based control systems, a further distinction can be made according to the attention patterns of senior managers and the effects of these attention patterns on the formation and implementation of strategy.

The final exhibit provides a checklist of the attributes of a sound internal control system. This system does not relate directly to strategy formation and implementation, but it is essential in any business, large or small, in order to ensure that assets are secure and management information is reliable. Without this assurance, managers cannot rely on the control levers.

Lever #1: Beliefs Systems

WHAT   explicit set of beliefs that define basic values, purpose, and direction, including how value is created; level of desired performance; and human relationships

WHY   to provide momentum and guidance to opportunity-seeking behaviors

HOW   mission statements
vision statements
credos
statements of purpose

WHEN   opportunities expand dramatically
top managers desire to change strategic direction
top managers desire to energize workforce

WHO   senior managers personally write substantive drafts
staff groups facilitate communication, feedback, and awareness surveys

---

Lever #2: Boundary Systems

WHAT   formally stated rules, limits, and proscriptions tied to defined sanctions and credible threat of punishment

WHY   to allow individual creativity within defined limits of freedom

HOW   codes of business conduct
strategic planning systems
asset acquisition systems
operational guidelines

WHEN   Business Conduct Boundaries: when reputation costs are high
Strategic Boundaries: when excessive search and experimentation risk dissipating the resources of the firm

WHO   senior managers formulate with the technical assistance of staff experts (e.g., lawyers) and personally mete out punishment
staff groups monitor compliance

Lever #3: Diagnostic Control Systems

WHAT feedback systems that monitor organizational outcomes and correct deviations from preset standards of performance

Examples: profit plans and budgets
goals and objectives systems
project monitoring systems
brand revenue monitoring systems
strategic planning systems

WHY to allow effective resource allocation
to define goals
to provide motivation
to establish guidelines for corrective action
to allow *ex post* evaluation
to free scarce management attention

HOW set standards
measure outputs
link incentives to goal achievement

WHEN performance standards can be preset
outputs can be measured
feedback information can be used to influence or correct deviations from standard
process or output is a critical performance variable

WHO senior managers set or negotiate goals, receive and review exception reports, follow-up significant exceptions
staff groups maintain systems, gather data, and prepare exception reports

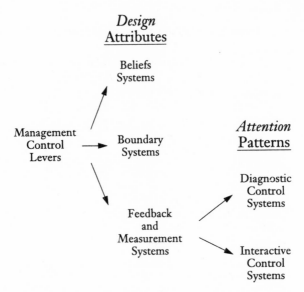

Figure A.1 Distinguishing Features of Control Levers

Lever #4: Interactive Control Systems

WHAT   control systems that managers use to involve themselves regularly and personally in the decision activities of subordinates

          Examples: profit planning systems
                     project management systems
                     brand revenue systems
                     intelligence systems

WHY   to focus organizational attention on strategic uncertainties and provoke the emergence of new initiatives and strategies

HOW   ensure that data generated by the system becomes an important and recurring agenda in discussions with subordinates
ensure that the system is the focus of regular attention by managers throughout the organization
participate in face-to-face meetings with subordinates
continually challenge and debate data, assumptions, and action plans

WHEN   strategic uncertainties require search for disruptive change and opportunities

WHO   senior managers actively use the system and assign subjective, effort-based rewards
staff groups act as facilitators

Foundation: Internal Control Systems

(Internal control systems are not among levers used by managers to control strategy. They are, however, fundamental to ensuring the integrity of data used in all other control systems. For this reason, managers must ensure that internal controls are adequate.)

WHAT   systems that safeguard assets from theft or accidental loss and ensure reliable accounting records and financial information systems

WHY   to prevent inefficiency in transaction processing, flawed decisions based on inaccurate data, fraud

HOW   Structural Safeguards
active audit committee of the board
independent internal audit function
segregation of duties
defined levels of authorization
restricted access to valuable assets

Staff Safeguards
adequate expertise and training for all accounting, control, and internal audit staff
sufficient resources
rotation in key jobs

Systems Safeguards
complete and accurate record keeping
adequate documentation and audit trail
relevant and timely management reporting
restricted access to information systems and data bases

WHEN   at all times in all businesses

WHO   staff professionals (trained accountants, independent auditors)
managers usually should not spend much time designing or reviewing the details of internal controls

Appendix B
Use and Misuse
of Information Technology

No one would dispute that computer-based information systems are essential to the operation of modern businesses. These systems generate virtually all transaction and production information in large organizations. The influence of technology on management practice, however, has been uneven. Although there has been eager anticipation of a revolution in management practice as a result of information technology, this revolution has been slow to materialize. Almost twenty years ago, Chris Argyris noted:

In a recent review of the literature on management information systems implementation, I found the major theme to be unmet expectations and disappointments, especially when management information systems technology was used to deal with the more complex and ill-structured problems faced by organizations (1977, 113).

Advances in technology and experience in implementation do not appear to have eradicated these problems. In a study of information usage in twelve manufacturing companies, McKinnon and Bruns echo an all too familiar theme:

The patterns of use we observed support a conclusion that information systems and personal computers have been put in place because technology has allowed them to be, rather than because of needs or consideration of the value of technology to enhance connections or relationships. As a result, not all managers have embraced the new technology and learned to use it effectively. Some who have tried to use the new technology have given up because other methods of getting information have a higher value-to-effort ratio in their jobs or experience (1992, 190).

McKinnon and Bruns conclude that much of the information delivered by information technology systems is not useful to managers, and therefore not used, because of deficiencies in timeliness, accuracy, and relevance.

Why is the information delivered by new technology useful to managers in some instances and not in others? I believe that senior managers have been slow to adopt information technology, not because of limitations in the technology per se, but because the designers of these systems do not understand how senior managers use information for control purposes. For information technology to be useful, it must be able to increase return-on-management (ROM) by leveraging scarce organizational attention. The challenge is to match the power of information technology to the control needs of managers, recognizing that different levers of control require different configurations of information systems.

Two related attributes of information, developed analytically by Boisot (1986), are especially relevant to the analysis of the communication and control needs of senior managers: *information codification* and *information diffusion*.

Information codification refers to the structuring of information by categorizing and compressing data. Descriptive statistics—mean, mode, and standard deviation—and financial statement information—revenues, expenses, and gross margins—represent highly codified information. Codified information is obtained by compressing raw data and categorizing these data into aggregated formats. In contrast, gossip about a new technology is difficult to codify because it is vague, ambiguous, and dependent upon context.

Information diffusion refers to the degree of information sharing within an organization. Diffusion is high if the information can be transmitted easily to everyone in the organization; diffusion is low if the information is available to only a small subset of the organization. An income statement can be diffused easily throughout an organization. Gossip about a new technology cannot be diffused easily because the transmittal of perceptions, especially nuances and hunches, requires face-to-face retelling of the story and the circumstances that led to it.

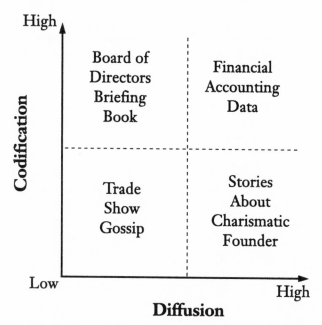

Figure B.1   Examples of the Interaction of Codification and Diffusion

Codification and diffusion of information are often interdependent (Figure B.1). Generally, the more that information can be codified, the more readily it can be diffused in an impersonal way. Accounting data, for example, can be compressed and structured according to a predefined code of accounts; these data are then easily and rapidly diffused inside the organization. Uncodified information, in contrast, is difficult to diffuse because accurate transmission depends on passing along the context within which the information was gathered and should be interpreted.

There are exceptions. Some information can be highly codified but still require face-to-face meetings to be interpreted and understood. The briefing book supplied to a board member in advance of a scheduled directors meeting is an example. The data are coded, but presentations, personal interaction, and discussion are necessary to fully comprehend the meaning of the data (Boisot 1986). Finally, some informal information is uncodified but widely diffused. A story about the company's founder, for example, may be retold countless times as a way of influencing the culture of the organization.

Manipulating the coding and diffusion of strategic information is a serious constraint to effective strategy formation and implementation. The more strategic the data, the more difficult it usually is to code for transmission within the organization. As a result, senior management preferences often cannot be easily diffused throughout the organization. Subtle intelligence data—such as those gathered at a trade show—are also difficult to diffuse widely and accurately. On the other hand, data that can be codified and diffused easily—sales transaction processing records—may provide information on variables that have little relevance to strategy formation and implementation.

To be useful to senior managers, information technology must provide information channels that are both efficient and effective in codifying and diffusing strategic information. Unfortunately, designers have failed to exploit the potential of technology to ease the constraints imposed by limits of codification and diffusion and scarce management attention.

An obvious solution is to use advances in technology to codify greater amounts of information and diffuse that information widely. But codifying greater amounts of information and diffusing the information widely does not increase ROM. In order to understand how to design information systems that permit changes in codification and diffusion and, at the same time, leverage scarce attention, we must revisit the levers of control.

Levers of Control and
Information Technology

Beliefs systems, boundary systems, diagnostic control systems, and interactive control systems have different informational purposes and therefore require differing degrees of codification and diffusion. Organizational constraints of time, distance, and space often limit the ability of managers to codify and diffuse information in the most effective way. Information technology, if properly designed, can overcome these constraints and allow the control levers to function more effectively. Exhibit B.1 summarizes the systems, the degree of codification and diffusion required, and the information technology required and available to overcome constraints.

Beliefs systems in the forms of mission statements and credos are used by top managers to transmit beliefs and values to lower levels of the organization and to provide an overall sense of direction and

	Beliefs Systems	Boundary Systems	Diagnostic Control Systems	Interactive Control Systems
Purpose	Stimulate search	Stake out strategic domain	Communicate critical performance targets and monitor progress against plans	Focus organizational search activities and information sharing on strategic uncertainties
Desired Codification	Uncoded, highly personal	Uncoded, unambiguous	Coded to measure and monitor critical performance variables	Semicoded to transform raw data into easily accessible formats
Desired Diffusion	Entire organization on a periodic basis	Entire business unit on a periodic basis	Responsible managers on an exception basis	Entire management group on an ongoing basis
Information Technology	Overcome distance and time to diffuse personalized message widely	Ensure unambiguous message is internalized	Increase efficiency and effectiveness of (1) critical performance measurement (2) transmission of exception information	Increase access to real time data about market dynamics; action planning and scenario testing
Examples	Audio-video conferencing Electronic mail	"Mischarging is illegal" on data entry screen	Color-coded exception reporting Drill-down matrix Balanced scorecard reports	Data base access to market trends, profitability models, internal technology projects

Exhibit B.1 Information Attributes of the Levers of Control

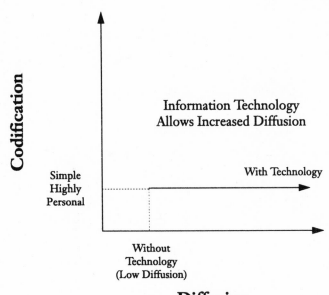

Diffusion

Figure B.2   Beliefs Systems and Information Technology

stimulate search behavior. The information transmitted through beliefs systems is ambiguous enough to allow organizational participants to use the information in ways that relate to their tasks. To inspire search activity, the information must be delivered in an inspirational way. Thus, the information must be delivered either directly through personal speeches or interpersonal contact or in ways that make it clear to recipients that the beliefs represent the fundamental values of senior managers.

This information, therefore, must be uncoded and highly personalized. At the same time, to be effective in stimulating search activity, the information must be diffused as widely as possible. When organizations are small and organizational participants work together closely, these joint demands can be met with little problem. Uncoded data can be diffused widely as senior managers present their message personally to all employees. With dispersed organizations, however, limits on the codification of the information limit the ability of senior managers to diffuse it widely through the organization. Managers are constrained by the number of people they can reach personally. As Figure B.2 illustrates, information technology can overcome obstacles of distance and time to make uncodified information more easily diffused. Video-conferencing, voice-mail, and electronic-mail allow senior managers to personalize and diffuse information related to core values and beliefs. A sense of immediacy and intimacy can be created that allows highly personalized messages to be dispersed to all members of the organization simultaneously. Thus, information technology can leverage small amounts of top management attention to communicate beliefs systems in a highly personal way.

Boundary systems communicate behavioral and strategic domains and thereby demarcate search activity. The information transmitted through boundary systems is unambiguous and typically rule-based (e.g., do not pursue opportunities in markets in which we cannot hold a number one or number two position within five years). Although the information does not need to be personalized, organizational participants must believe that the boundaries are important to top managers and are, therefore, to be respected.

Only those organizational participants who could face choices that pose risks to the business need know business conduct and strategic boundaries. Rules on dealing with government agencies, for example, must be transmitted to those segments that interact or sell to the government. Strategic boundaries—which business segments to avoid—are tailored to individual business units.

Although the information contained in boundary systems is uncoded, it does not need to be personalized. Instead, the threat of sanction is sufficient to attract attention and ensure compliance. As organizations become larger and more decentralized, however, communicating boundaries becomes more difficult. Periodic memoranda and mailings may fail to gain attention as they compete with more pressing day-to-day tasks and problems. Information technology can allow boundaries to be communicated continually to organizational participants, in some cases by automating boundary checks. To do so, there must be limited increases in both codification and diffusion and greater monitoring by technology staff groups (Figure B.3). However, these enhancements do not require additional senior management attention.

At a business that suffered a scandal caused by the manipulation of accounting records by junior managers, the bottom of every computer screen now contains the message, "Mischarging is Illegal." At a more strategic level, computer software can scan planning assumptions to test whether or not critical strategic boundaries (e.g., risk exposure in a bank) are in danger of being violated. Thus, without constant intervention by senior managers, information technology can

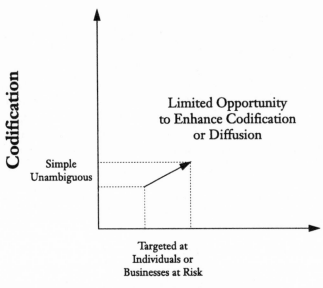

Diffusion

Figure B.3   Boundary Systems and Information Technology

provide assurance that strategic and business conduct boundaries are being communicated and monitored.

Senior managers use diagnostic control systems to communicate critical performance targets and monitor progress in achieving plans. Information about intended strategy, plans, and targets cascades down the organization from higher to lower levels. As it does so, the information is disaggregated in a sequential process that allows lower level goals and targets to contribute to the overall strategy of the business. Business plans, goals and objectives systems, and budgets are diagnostic control systems that provide resources, coordinate activities, and motivate performance to achieve predetermined outcomes.

The information transmitted through diagnostic control systems is highly coded. Planning guidelines, budgets, and other diagnostic control systems impose uniform information structures that are often transformations of data from the financial accounting system. Because higher levels of the organization receive increasingly aggegated data, some training and skill is necessary to decode and understand the information, but this training is usually a prerequisite for advancement to general management positions. Staff experts (accountants, sales planners, information technologists), who are able to design so-phisticated and complex models to track and benchmark critical performance variables, maintain these systems, thus conserving the attention of senior managers and permitting management-by-exception.

Information technology can dramatically increase both the efficiency and effectiveness of codification in diagnostic control systems (Figure B.4). Thus, it can increase the ability of managers to monitor the performance of subordinates while reducing or eliminating the need for personal interaction (Zuboff 1988, 323). In terms of strategy, advanced information technology allows codification of measures relating to critical performance variables and the automation of early warning messages when targets are in jeopardy. This information technology allows more variables to be monitored and permits a balanced scorecard approach that includes financial, customer, internal business, and innovation measures (Kaplan and Norton 1992). Executive information systems permit "drill-down" access to variance information. Color-coded computer screen matrixes can highlight exception reporting. A variety of key measures can be scanned on a regular basis to ensure that critical performance variables are on target. For large, multidomestic companies competing in multiple markets, these systems are essential windows into complex business operations.

To conserve organizational attention, the diffusion of diagnostic control information is often constrained by design. Senior managers can, for example, restrict access to information relevant to an individual manager's responsibilities. Functional and business area managers of a strategic business unit receive only data relating to operations under their responsibility. Wider access risks organizational distraction and introduces data security concerns. Thus, diffusion is limited by design, not by technology (Simons 1992; Simons and Bartlett 1992).

While information technology offers significant opportunities to improve diagnostic control systems, designers must remember that the purpose of these systems is to allow the achievement of goals and objectives without constant senior management attention. Executive information systems can upset the ability of diagnostic control systems to conserve organizational attention as they allow access to detailed data at very low organizational levels. Staff designers encourage senior managers to "drill down" in the organization data base to monitor lower level activities. At first, this seems desirable, but reflection about the purpose of diagnostic systems suggests substantial risks.

What happens when a division manager identifies an unfavorable

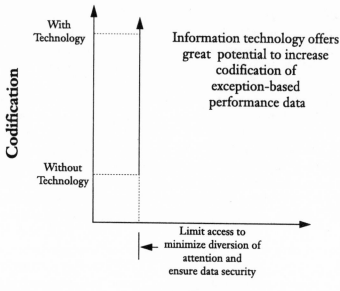

Diffusion

Figure B.4   Diagnostic Control Systems and Information Technology

monthly variance in a small expense center? If he or she picks up the telephone and calls the supervisor involved, two things may happen. At best, the supervisor will explain that the variance is due to timing differences that caused expenses to be unusually high this month. It is more probable, however, that the supervisor will inform subordinates that the division manager is upset about the variance and ask them to find a way to eliminate it, even though they are already aware of it and would have taken actions to correct it if circumstances did not change.[1] In this type of surveillance environment, subordinates may spend an inordinate amount of time monitoring minute diagnostic variables so they will not be caught unaware by the questioning of senior managers.

By nature, diagnostic control systems are self-correcting feedback systems. Engineers understand that the system will become unstable if a feedback signal is continually perturbed before the system has time to assimilate the information and self-correct. Information

[1] For a discussion of the implications of this problem in changing traditional organizational power relationships, see Zuboff (1988), pp. 338–41.

technology can allow senior managers to perturb inherently self-correcting control processes and thus divert organizational attention in unproductive ways.

Interactive control systems are used by senior managers to stimulate dialogue and debate about strategic uncertainties. Any management control system can be used interactively by focusing intense and recurring management attention on that system. Recurring attention will cause a cascading effect as managers throughout the organization meet to gather and interpret data in anticipation of a search for understanding from peers and superiors. An interactive control system motivates the search for information about strategic uncertainties as well as the development of new action plans and, sometimes, new strategies. Information flows are up, down, and across the organization as information is collected, shared, communicated, and debated.

Information transmitted through interactive control systems is semicoded. The interactive control system provides structure for data compression and categorization (e.g., profit planning systems), but data transmitted by the system serve primarily as catalysts to promote face-to-face dialogue and debate about the meaning of information and appropriate action plans. Because debate focuses on the meaning of the information rather than on how it was calculated and transformed, interactive control systems must be simple so that individuals throughout the organization can understand them.

The diffusion of information for an interactive system is greater than diffusion for a diagnostic control system. Interactive control systems are intended to promote dialogue and information sharing and are designed to be important data sources to the entire management group of a business, even though interactive control system information may be reported formally to only a subset of managers (Figure B.5).

Advances in information technology have the potential to improve the power of interactive systems in three ways. First, computer information systems have the ability to take complex data and transform them into visual patterns and charts that are easy to comprehend. Thus, these systems allow complex data to become part of interactive control systems. Second, the proliferation of networked personal computers allows relevant market information to be transmitted, shared, and discussed rapidly. Profit planning systems can be pushed lower in the organization. Point-of-sale data collection devices can collect and quickly disseminate real-time data about customer buying patterns and the effectiveness of promotions and pricing

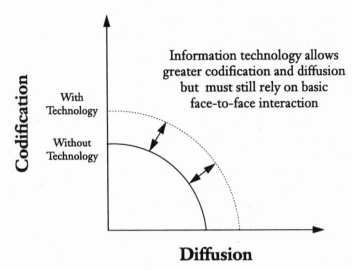

Diffusion

Figure B.5 Interactive Control Systems and Information Technology

changes. Third, advances in data base management allow managers
to ask "what-if" questions that can assess scenarios associated with
suggested action plans. Data bases facilitate reforecasting of data and
market dynamics. Advances in information technology allow *pro forma*
calculations to be made easily and rapidly.

All of these enhancements allow interactive control systems to
contain more relevant, timely, and sensitive data about strategic uncertainties and, at the same time, keep the data simple and easy to
access. Better data about strategic uncertainties allows better returns
for the management attention that is devoted to these systems. Even
so, interactive control systems rely on face-to-face discussions. Thus,
the information in an interactive system must remain semi-coded.
Information technology specialists often prefer more codified media
where the power of technology allows rapid and efficient diffusion of
information. Too often, however, this removes interaction from the
communication channel. Research indicates that human interaction
is critical to effective control and management. In a study entitled
"Impediments to the Use of Management Information," Mintzberg
stated:

A . . . weakness of the [formal management information system] is that in
relying on documentation it loses much information *verbal channels* can provide. Specifically, in face-to-face contact the manager can "read" facial ex-
pression, gesture, tone of voice, and so on. Documents are sterile by compar-

ison. Furthermore, verbal channels allow for the immediate feedback and interaction which managers apparently find so important. (1975, 3–4; italics in original)

In a recent study of electronic mail use by managers, McKenney, Zack, and Doherty noted that face-to-face communications were preferred to electronic mail for complex problem solving:

We identified a fundamental trade-off between the efficiency of communication provided by electronic mail in well-defined contexts versus the ability to build a shared understanding and definition of the situation or task via face-to-face communication. Face-to-face communication (both one-on-one and scheduled meetings) provided the richness to support the level of interactivity, immediacy of feedback, and social presence required to resolve equivocal issues or issues requiring a complex set of exchanges, and created a shared understanding in the group so that a focused and structured communication-in-context could occur. (1992, 283)

Electronic media are neither appropriate nor desirable for certain types of control systems. Nohria and Eccles (1992) argue that face-to-face communication becomes increasingly important as situations increase in uncertainty, ambiguity, and risk. In these situations, electronic communication cannot provide a meaningful substitute. Experience will determine whether video-conferencing and other emerging technologies that combine digital computing power with audiovisual capabilities will be able to ease these constraints.

The way in which senior managers use formal systems to control strategy is a critical factor in the design of information technology systems. Given the severe attention constraints of senior managers, failure to recognize different usage patterns can only result in managers abandoning the new information technology systems that are offered to them in favor of more traditional ways of collecting and communicating information.

References

Ackoff, R. L. 1971. Towards a System of Systems Concepts. *Management Science* 17(11):661–671.

Amabile, T. M., and S. S. Gryskiewicz. 1988. Creative Human Resources in the R & D Laboratory: How Environment and Personality Affect Innovation. In *Handbook for Creative and Innovative Managers*, ed. R. L. Kuhn. New York: McGraw-Hill.

Amey, L. R. 1979. *Budget Planning and Control Systems*. Marshfield, Mass.: Pitman.

Andrews, K. R. 1989. Ethics in Practice. *Harvard Business Review* 67(5): 99–104.

Anthony, R. N. 1965. *Planning and Control Systems: A Framework for Analysis*. Boston: Division of Research, Graduate School of Business Administration, Harvard University.

———. 1988. *The Management Control Function*. Boston: Harvard Business School Press.

Argyris, C. 1952. *The Impact of Budgets on People*. New York: The Controllership Foundation.

———. 1973. Some Limits of Rational Man Organization Theory. *Public Administration Review* 33(3):253–67.

———. 1977. Organizational Learning and Management Information Systems. *Accounting, Organizations and Society* 2(2):113–23.

———. 1985. *Strategy, Change and Defensive Routines*. Marshfield, Mass.: Pitman.

————. 1990a. The Dilemma of Implementing Controls: The Case of Managerial Accounting. *Accounting, Organizations and Society* 15(6):503–511.

————. 1990b. *Overcoming Organizational Defenses: Facilitating Organizational Learning.* Needham, Mass.: Allyn and Bacon.

Argyris, C., and D. Schön. 1978. *Organizational Learning.* Reading, Mass.: Addison-Wesley.

Arrow, K. J. 1974. *The Limits of Organization.* New York: W.W. Norton.

Ashforth, B. E., and F. Mael. 1989. Social Identity Theory and the Organization. *Academy of Management Review* 14(1):20–39.

Baldwin, Y. C., and K. B. Clark. 1992. Capabilities and Capital Investment: New Perspectives on Capital Budgeting. *Journal of Applied Corporate Finance.* 5(2):67–82.

Barnard, C. I. [1938] 1968. *The Functions of the Executive.* Cambridge, Mass.: Harvard University Press.

Barney, J. B., and W. G. Ouchi, eds. 1986. *Organizational Economics.* San Francisco, Calif.: Jossey-Bass.

Barrett, M. E., and L. B. Fraser. 1977. Conflicting Roles in Budgeting for Operations. *Harvard Business Review* 55(4):137–46.

Baruch, H. 1980. The Audit Committee: A Guide For Directors. *Harvard Business Review* 58(3):174–86.

Birnberg, J. G., L. Turopolec, and S. M. Young. 1983. The Organizational Context of Accounting. *Accounting, Organizations and Society* 8(2/3): 111–29.

Boisot, M. H. 1986. Markets and Hierarchies in a Cultural Perspective. *Organization Studies* 7:135–58.

Bower, J. L. [1970] 1986. *Managing the Resource Allocation Decision.* Boston: Harvard Business School Press.

Brenner, S. N., and E. A. Molander. 1977. Is the Ethics of Business Changing? *Harvard Business Review* 55(1):57–71.

Brooks, L. J., and V. Fortunato. 1991. Discipline at the ICAO. *CA Magazine* 124(5):40–43.

Brown, D. [1957] 1977. *Some Reminiscences of an Industrialist.* Easton, Pennsylvania: Hive Publishing.

Brown, W. 1960. *Explorations in Management.* New York: Wiley.

Brownell, P. 1982. Participation in the Budgeting Process—When it Works and When it Doesn't. *Journal of Accounting Literature* 1(spring):124–53.

Brownell, P., and M. McInnes. 1986. Budgetary Participation, Motivation, and Managerial Performance. *The Accounting Review* 61(October): 587–600.

Bruns, W. J., Jr., and P. J. Murray. 1989. Roy Rogers Restaurants. Case Study 9-189-100. Boston: Harvard Business School.

Bruns, W. J., Jr., and K. A. Merchant. 1990. The Dangerous Morality of Managing Earnings. *Management Accounting* 72(2):22–25.

Burgelman, R. 1983a. A Model of the Interaction of Strategic Behavior, Corporate Context, and the Concept of Strategy. *Academy of Management Review* 8(1):61–90.

———. 1983b. A Process Model of Internal Corporate Venturing in a Diversified Major Firm. *Administrative Science Quarterly* 28(2):223–44.

———. 1983c. Corporate Entrepreneurship and Strategic Management: Insights from a Process Study. *Management Science*. 29(12):1349–64.

———. 1991. Intraorganizational Ecology of Strategy Making and Organizational Adaptation: Theory and Field Research. *Organization Science* 2(3): 239–62.

Burns, T., and G. M. Stalker. 1961. *The Management of Innovation*. London: Tavistock.

Burt, R. S. 1992. The Social Structure of Competition. In *Networks and Organizations: Structure, Form, and Action*, eds. N. Nohria and R. G. Eccles. Boston: Harvard Business School Press.

Carroll, A. B. 1975. Managerial Ethics: A Post-Watergate Review. *Business Horizons* 18(2):75–80.

Carroll, S. J., and H. L. Tosi. 1973. *Management by Objectives: Applications and Research*. New York: Macmillan.

Chandler, A. D., Jr. 1962. *Strategy and Structure: Chapters in the History of the American Industrial Enterprise*. Cambridge, Mass.: MIT Press.

Christenson, C. 1972. The Power of Negative Thinking. Working paper 72–41. Graduate School of Business Administration, Harvard University, Boston.

Cohen, M. D., J. D. March, and J. P. Olsen. 1972. A Garbage Can Model of Organizational Choice. *Administrative Quarterly* 17(1):1–26.

Coleman, J. S. 1990. *Foundations of Social Theory*. Cambridge, Mass.: Harvard University Press, Belknap Press.

Cyert, R. M. 1990. Defining Leadership and Explicating the Process. *Nonprofit Management & Leadership* 1(1):29–38.

Cyert, R. M., and J. G. March. 1963. *A Behavioral Theory of the Firm*. Englewood Cliffs, N.J.: Prentice Hall.

Daft, R. L., and S. W. Becker. 1978. *The Innovative Organization*. New York: Elsevier.

Daniel, D. R. 1966. Reorganizing for Results. *Harvard Business Review* 44(6): 96–104.

Dearden, J. 1969. The Case Against ROI Control. *Harvard Business Review* 47(3):124–35.

Deci, E. L., and R. M. Ryan. 1985. *Intrinsic Motivation and Self-Determination in Human Behavior*. New York: Plenum.

Dent, J. F. 1991. Accounting and Organizational Cultures: A Field Study of the Emergence of a New Organizational Reality. *Accounting, Organizations and Society* 16(8):705–32.

DiMaggio, P. J., and W. W. Powell. 1983. The Iron Cage Revisited: Institutional Isomorphism and Collective Rationality in Organizational Fields. *American Sociological Review* 48(April):147–60.

Donaldson, G., and J. W. Lorsch. 1983. *Decision Making at the Top*. New York: Basic.

Drucker, P. E. 1989. What Business Can Learn from Nonprofits. *Harvard Business Review* 67(4):88–93.

Eccles, R. G. 1991. The Performance Measurement Manifesto. *Harvard Business Review* 69(1):131–37.

Ettlie, J. E., W. P. Bridges, and R. D. O'Keefe. 1984. Organization Strategy and Structural Differences for Radical Versus Incremental Innovation. *Management Science* 30(6):682–95.

Fama, E. F., and M. C. Jensen. 1983. Separation of Ownership and Control. *Journal of Law and Economics* 26(2):301–25.

Feldman, M. S., and J. G. March. 1981. Information in Organizations as Signal and Symbol. *Administrative Science Quarterly* 26(2):171–86.

Frank, R. H. 1988. *Passions Within Reason: The Strategic Role of Emotions*. New York: Norton.

Gabarro, J. J. 1987. *The Dynamics of Taking Charge*. Boston: Harvard Business School Press.

Galbraith, J. R. 1977. *Organization Design*. Reading, Mass.: Addison-Wesley.

Gatewood, R. D., and A. B. Carroll. 1991. Assessment of Ethical Performance of Organization Members: A Conceptual Framework. *Academy of Management Review* 16(4):667–90.

Gellerman, S. W. 1986. Why "Good" Managers Make Bad Ethical Choices. *Harvard Business Review* 64(4):85–90.

Geneen, H. 1984. *Managing*. New York: Avon Books.

Ghemawat, P. 1991. *Commitment: The Dynamics of Strategy*. New York: The Free Press.

Gorlin, R. A. 1986. *Codes of Professional Responsibility*. Washington, D.C.: The Bureau of National Affairs.

Govindarajan, V., and A. K. Gupta. 1985. Linking Control Systems to Business Unit Strategy: Impact on Performance. *Accounting, Organizations and Society* 10(1):51–66.

Greiner, L. E., and A. Bhambri. 1989. New CEO Intervention and Dynamics of Deliberate Strategic Change. *Strategic Management Journal* 10(Summer Special Issue):67–86.

Hambrick, D. C., and A. A. Cannella. 1989. Strategy Implementation as Substance and Selling. *The Academy of Management Executive* 3(4): 278–85.

Hannan, M. T., and J. Freeman. 1984. Structural Inertia and Organizational Change. *American Sociological Review* 49:149–64.

Hayek, F. A. 1978. The Confusion About "Planning." In *New Studies in Philosophy, Politics, Economics, and the History of Ideas*. Chicago: University of Chicago Press.

Hedberg, B., and S. Jönsson. 1978. Designing Semi-Confusing Information Systems for Organizations in Changing Environments. *Accounting, Organizations and Society* 3(1):47–64.

Hedberg, B., P. C. Nystrom, and W. H. Starbuck. 1976. Camping on Seesaws: Prescriptions for a Self-Designing Organization. *Administrative Science Quarterly* 21:41–65.

Helmich, D. L., and W. B. Brown. 1972. Successor Type and Organizational Change in the Corporate Enterprise. *Administrative Science Quarterly* 17:371–81.

Herzberg, F. 1966. *Work and the Nature of Man*. Cleveland, Ohio: World Publishing.

Hofstede, G. 1968. *The Game of Budget Control*. London: Tavistock.

Holloway, D. 1990. The Catastrophe and After. *The New York Review of Books*, 19 July, 5.

Holmström, B. 1979. Moral Hazards and Observability. *Bell Journal of Economics* 10(1):74–91.

Hopwood, A. G. 1974. *Accounting and Human Behavior*. Englewood Cliffs, N.J.: Prentice Hall.

———. 1987. The Archaeology of Accounting Systems. *Accounting, Organizations and Society* 12(3):207–34.

Iacocca, L. 1984. *Iacocca: an Autobiography*. New York: Bantam Books.

Ijiri, Y. 1975. *Theory of Accounting Measurement*. Studies in Accounting Research #10. Sarasota, Fla: American Accounting Association.

Institute of Management Accountants (formerly National Association of Accountants). 1983. Statements on Management Accounting: Standards of Ethical Conduct for Management Accountants, Statement No. 1C. New York.

Jensen, M. C. 1983. Organization Theory and Methodology. *The Accounting Review* 57(April):319–39.

———. 1993. The Modern Industrial Revolution, Exit, and the Failure of Internal Control Systems. *The Journal of Finance* 48(3):831–80.

Jensen, M. C., and W. H. Meckling. 1976. Theory of the Firm: Managerial Behavior, Agency Costs, and Ownership Structure. *Journal of Financial Economics* 3(4):305–60.

Johnson, H. T., and R. S. Kaplan. 1987. *Relevance Lost: The Rise and Fall of Management Accounting*. Boston: Harvard Business School Press.

Kanter, R. M. 1977. *Men and Women of the Corporation*. New York: Basic Books.

———. 1991. Championing Change: An Interview with Bell Atlantic's CEO Raymond Smith. *Harvard Business Review* 69(1):119–30.

Kaplan, R. S. 1984. The Evolution of Management Accounting. *The Accounting Review* 59(July):390–418.

Kaplan, R. S., and D. P. Norton. 1992. The Balanced Scorecard—Measures That Drive Performance. *Harvard Business Review* 70(1):71–79.

Kaufman, H. 1960. *The Forest Ranger: A Study in Administrative Behavior.* Baltimore: Johns Hopkins Press.

Keller, M. 1989. *Rude Awakening: The Rise, Fall, and Struggle for Recovery of General Motors.* New York: William Morrow.

Kenis, I. 1979. Effects of Budgetary Goal Characteristics on Managerial Attitudes and Performance. *The Accounting Review* 54(October):707–21.

Kohlberg, L., and E. Turiel. 1973. *Moralization: The Cognitive Development Approach.* New York: Holt, Rinehart & Winston.

Kotter, J. P. 1982. *The General Managers.* New York: The Free Press.

———. 1990. *A Force for Change.* New York: The Free Press.

Kuhn, A. J. 1986. *GM Passes Ford, 1918–1938: Designing the General Motors Performance-Control System.* University Park, Penn.: Pennsylvania State University Press.

Langer, E. J. 1989. *Mindfulness.* Reading, Mass.: Addison-Wesley.

Lawler, E. E., III. 1972. Secrecy and the Need to Know. In *Readings in Managerial Motivation and Compensation*, ed. M. Dunnette, R. House, and H. Tosi. East Lansing: Michigan State University Press.

———. 1973. *Motivation in Work Organizations.* Monterey, Calif.: Brooks/Cole.

———. 1976. Control Systems in Organizations. In *Handbook of Industrial and Organizational Psychology*, ed. M. Dunnette. Chicago: Rand McNally.

Lawler, E. E., III, and J. G. Rhode. 1976. *Information and Control in Organizations.* Santa Monica, Calif.: Goodyear.

Lawrence, P. R., and D. Dyer. 1983. *Renewing American Industry.* New York: The Free Press.

Leblebici, H., and G. R. Salancik. 1982. Stability in Interorganizational Exchanges: Rulemaking Processes of the Chicago Board of Trade. *Administrative Science Quarterly* 27:227–42.

Levitt, B., and J. G. March. 1988. Organizational Learning. *American Review of Sociology* 14:319–40.

Levitt, T. 1960. Marketing Myopia. *Harvard Business Review* 38(4):45–56.

Likert, R. 1961. *New Patterns of Management.* New York: McGraw Hill.

Locke, E. A., G. P. Latham, and M. Erez. 1988. The Determinants of Goal Commitment. *Academy of Management Review* 13(1):23–39.

Lorange, P. 1980. *Corporate Planning: An Executive Viewpoint.* Englewood Cliffs, N.J.: Prentice Hall.

Lorange, P., and M. S. Scott Morton. 1974. A Framework for Management Control. *Sloan Management Review* 16:41–56.

Lorange, P., M. S. Scott Morton, and S. Goshal. 1986. *Strategic Control.* St. Paul, Minn.: West.

McGregor, D. 1960. *The Human Side of Enterprise.* New York: McGraw Hill.

McKenney, J. L., M. H. Zack, and V. S. Doherty. 1992. Complementary Communication Media: A Comparison of Electronic Mail and Face-to-Face Communication in a Programming Team. In *Networks and Organizations; Structure, Form, and Action,* ed. N. Nohria and R. G. Eccles. Boston: Harvard Business School Press.

McKinnon, S. M., and W. J. Bruns, Jr. 1992. *The Information Mosaic.* Boston: Harvard Business School Press.

March, J. D., ed. 1988. *Decisions and Organizations.* New York: Basil Blackwell.

March, J. D., and R. Weissinger-Baylon. 1986. *Ambiguity and Command: Organizational Perspectives on Military Decision Making.* Marshfield, Mass.: Pitman.

Maslow, A. H. 1943. A Theory of Human Motivation. *Psychological Review* 50:370–96.

———. 1954. *Motivation and Personality.* New York: Harper & Row.

Mayo, E. [1949] 1975. *The Social Problems of an Industrial Civilization.* London: Routledge & Kegan Paul.

Mercer, D. 1987. *IBM: How the World's Most Successful Corporation Is Managed.* London: Kogan Page.

Merchant, K. A. 1985. *Control in Business Organizations.* Marshfield, Mass.: Pitman.

———. 1989. *Rewarding Results: Motivating Profit Center Managers.* Boston: Harvard Business School Press.

———. 1990. The Effects of Financial Controls on Data Manipulation and Management Myopia. *Accounting, Organizations and Society* 15(4):297–313.

Merchant, K. A., and R. Simons. 1986. Research and Control In Complex Organizations: An Overview. *Journal of Accounting Literature* 5:183–203.

Meyer, J. W., and B. Rowan. 1977. Institutionalized Organizations: Formal Structure as Myth and Ceremony. *American Journal of Sociology* 83(2): 340–363.

Meyer, H. H., E. Kay, and J. R. P. French. 1965. Split Roles in Performance Appraisal. *Harvard Business Review* 43(1):123–29.

Miller, D., and P. H. Friesen. 1984. *Organizations: A Quantum View.* Englewood Cliffs, N.J.: Prentice Hall.

Mintzberg, H. 1973. *The Nature of Managerial Work.* New York: Harper & Row.

———. 1975. *Impediments to the Use of Management Information.* New York: National Association of Accountants.

———. 1978. Patterns in Strategy Formation. *Management Science* 24(3): 934–48.

———. 1979. *The Structuring of Organizations*. Englewood Cliffs, N.J.: Prentice Hall.

———. 1987a. Five P's for Strategy. *California Management Review* 30(1): 11–24.

———. 1987b. Crafting Strategy. *Harvard Business Review* 65(4):66–75.

———. 1990. The Design School: Reconsidering the Basic Premises of Strategic Management. *Strategic Management Journal* 11(3):171–95.

———. 1994. *The Rise and Fall of Strategic Planning*. New York: The Free Press.

Mintzberg, H., and J. A. Waters. 1982. Tracking Strategy in an Entrepreneurial Firm. *Academy of Management Journal* 25(3):465–99.

———. 1985. Of Strategies, Deliberate and Emergent. *Strategic Management Journal* 6:257–72.

Morison, S. E., 1935. *The Founding of Harvard College*. Cambridge, Mass.: Harvard University Press.

Nelson, R. R., and S. G. Winter. 1982. *An Evolutionary Theory of Economic Change*. Cambridge, Mass.: Harvard University Press.

Nohria, N., and R. G. Eccles. 1992. Face-to-Face: Making Network Organizations Work. In *Networks and Organizations: Structure, Form, and Action*, eds. N. Nohria and R. G. Eccles. Boston: Harvard Business School Press.

Nonaka, Ikujiro. 1988. Toward Middle-Up-Down Management. *Sloan Management Review* 29(3):9–18.

Otley, D. T., and A. J. Berry. 1980. Control, Organization and Accounting. *Accounting, Organizations and Society* 5(2):231–46.

Ouchi, W. G. 1977. The Relationship Between Organizational Structure and Organizational Control. *Administrative Science Quarterly* 22:95–113.

Pascale, R. T. 1984. Perspectives on Strategy: The Real Story Behind Honda's Success. *California Management Review* 26(3):47–72.

Perrow, C. 1986. *Organizations: A Critical Essay*. 3d ed. New York: Random House.

Peters, T. J., and R. H. Waterman. 1982. *In Search of Excellence*. New York: Harper & Row.

Pettigrew, A. M. 1985. *The Awakening Giant: Continuity and Change in Imperial Chemical Industries*. Oxford: Basil Blackwell.

Porter, M. E. 1980. *Competitive Strategy: Techniques for Analyzing Industries and Competitors*. New York: The Free Press.

———. 1985. *Competitive Advantage*. New York: The Free Press.

———. 1990. *The Competitive Advantage of Nations*. New York: The Free Press.

———. 1992. Capital Disadvantage: America's Failing Capital Investment System. *Harvard Business Review* 70(5):65–82.

Quinn, J. B. 1977. Strategic Goals: Process and Politics. *Sloan Management Review* 19(1):21–37.

———. 1980. *Strategies for Change: Logical Incrementalism.* Homewood, Ill.: Irwin.

Rathe, A. W. 1960. Management Controls in Business. In *Management Control Systems*, ed. D. G. Malcolm and A. J. Rowe. New York: Wiley, 28–60.

Rich, A. J., C. S. Smith, and P. H. Mihalek. 1990. Are Corporate Codes of Conduct Effective? *Management Accounting* 72(3):34–35.

Ridgway, V. F. 1956. Dysfunctional Consequences of Performance Measurement. *Administrative Science Quarterly* 1:240–47.

Roberts, J. L. 1989. Credit Squeeze—Dun & Bradstreet Faces Flap Over How It Sells Reports on Business. *The Wall Street Journal*, 2 March, A1.

Roberts, J., and R. Scapens. 1985. Accounting Systems and Systems of Accountability—Understanding Accounting Practices in Their Organizational Contexts. *Accounting, Organizations and Society* 10(4):443–56.

Rosenbloom, R. S., ed. 1983. *Research on Technological Innovation, Management and Policy.* Greenwich, Conn.: JAI Press. Research Annual Series published in 1983 and subsequently in 1985, 1986, 1989, and 1993.

Ruckelshaus, William D. 1992. When Outsiders Get the Top Job. *New York Times*, 20 March, D1.

Schall, M. S. 1983. A Communication-Rules Approach to Organizational Culture. *Administrative Science Quarterly* 28:557–81.

Schroder, H. M., M. J. Driver, and S. Streufert. 1967. *Human Information Processing.* New York: Holt, Rinehart, and Winston.

Sculley, J. 1987. *Odyssey: Pepsi to Apple . . . A Journey of Adventure, Ideas, and the Future.* New York: Harper & Row.

Selznick, P. 1957. *Leadership in Administration: A Sociological Interpretation.* New York: Harper & Row.

Senge, P. M. 1990. The Leader's New Work: Building Learning Organizations. *Sloan Management Review* 32(1):7–23.

Simon, H. A. 1976. *Administrative Behavior: A Study of Decision-Making Processes in Administrative Situations.* 3d ed. New York: The Free Press.

Simons, R. 1987a. Accounting Control Systems and Business Strategy: An Empirical Analysis. *Accounting, Organizations and Society* 12(4):357–74.

———. 1987b. Planning, Control, and Uncertainty: A Process View. In *Accounting & Management: Field Study Perspectives*, ed. W. J. Bruns, Jr. and R. S. Kaplan. Boston: Harvard Business School Press.

———. 1987c. Codman & Shurtleff, Inc. Planning and Control System. Case Study 9-187-081. Boston: Harvard Business School.

———. 1989. General Electric: Compliance Systems. Case Study 1-189-081. Boston: Harvard Business School.

———. 1990. The Role of Management Control Systems in Creating Competitive Advantage: New Perspectives. *Accounting, Organizations and Society* 15(1/2):127–43.

———. 1991. Strategic Orientation and Top Management Attention to Control Systems. *Strategic Management Journal* 12:49–62.

———. 1992. Asea Brown Boveri: The ABACUS System. Case Study 9-192-140. Boston: Harvard Business School.

———. 1994. How New Top Managers Use Control Systems as Levers of Strategic Renewal. *Strategic Management Journal* 15:169–89.

Simons, R., and C. Bartlett. 1992. Asea Brown Boveri. Case Study 9-192-139. Boston: Harvard Business School.

Simons, R., and H. Weston. 1989. Automatic Data Processing: The EFS Decision. Case Study 9-190-059. Boston: Harvard Business School.

———. 1990a. IBM: "Make It Your Business." Case Study 9-190-137. Boston: Harvard Business School.

———. 1990b. Mary Kay Cosmetics: Sales Force Incentives. Case Study 9-190-103. Boston: Harvard Business School.

———. 1990c. Nordstrom: Dissension in the Ranks? Case Study 9-191-002. Boston: Harvard Business School.

———. 1990d. Turner Construction Company: Project Management System. Case Study 9-190-128. Boston: Harvard Business School.

———. 1990e. USA Today. Case Study 9-191-004. Boston: Harvard Business School.

Stedry, A., and E. Kay. 1966. The Effects of Goal Difficulty on Performance. *Behavioral Science* 11(6):459–70.

Steiner, G. A. 1979. *Strategic Planning: What Every Manager Must Know.* New York: The Free Press.

Sweeney, R. B., and H. L. Siers. 1990. Survey: Ethics in Corporate America. *Management Accounting* 71(12):34–40.

Taylor, F. W. 1911. *The Principles of Scientific Management.* New York: Harper.

Taylor, W. 1990. The Business of Innovation: An Interview with Paul Cook. *Harvard Business Review* 68(2):97–106.

Tiryakian, E. A. 1968. Typologies. In *International Encyclopedia of the Social Sciences*, ed. D. S. Sills. Vol. 16. New York: Macmillan.

Tosi, H. 1975. The Human Effects of Managerial Budgeting Systems. In *Managerial Accounting: The Behavioral Foundations*, ed. J. L. Livingstone. Columbus, Ohio: Grid.

Trice, H. M., and J. M. Beyer. 1991. Cultural Leadership in Organizations. *Organization Science* 2:149–69.

Tushman, M. L., W. H. Newman, and E. Romanelli. 1987. Convergence and Upheaval: Managing the Unsteady Pace of Organizational Evolution. *California Management Review* 29(1):29–44.

Umapathy, S. 1987. *Current Budgeting Practices in U.S. Industry: The State of the Art.* New York: Quorum Books.

Warren, D. L. 1984. Managing in Crisis: Nine Principles for Successful Transition. In *Managing Organizational Transitions*, ed. J. R. Kimberly and R. E. Quinn. Homewood, Ill.: Irwin.

Watson, T. J., Jr. 1963. *A Business and Its Beliefs: The Ideas That Helped Build IBM*. New York: McGraw-Hill.

———— with Peter Petre. 1990. *Father, Son & Co.: My Life at IBM and Beyond*. New York: Bantam Books.

Westley, F. R. 1990. Middle Managers and Stategy: Microdynamics of Inclusion. *Strategic Management Journal* 11:337–51.

Westley, F. R., and H. Mintzberg. 1989. Visionary Leadership and Strategic Management. *Strategic Management Journal* 10:17–32.

White, H. 1985. Agency as Control. In *Principals and Agents: The Structure of Business*, ed. J. W. Pratt and R. J. Zeckhauser. Boston: Harvard Business School Press.

Wiersema, M. F. 1992. Strategic Consequences of Executive Succession Within Diversified Firms. *Journal of Management Studies* 29(1):73–94.

Williamson, O. E. 1975. *Markets and Hierarchies: Analysis and Antitrust Implications*. New York: The Free Press.

Yin, T. 1992. Sears is Accused of Billing Fraud at Auto Centers. *The Wall Street Journal*, 16 June, B1.

Zuboff, S. 1988. *In the Age of the Smart Machine*. New York: Basic Books.

Index

Accountability, 42, 136–137, 165
Ackoff, R. L., 105
Andrews, K. R., 44, 56
Anthony, Robert, 18, 72, 76, 114
Argyris, Chris, 24, 25, 55, 69, 82, 87, 123, 124, 134, 183
Arrow, K. J., 14, 45
Ashforth, B. E., 37
Asset acquisition systems
  boundaries set by, 49, 51, 54–55, 179
  as diagnostic control systems, 87–89
Attention
  balancing opportunity and, 14–16
  boundary system incentives and, 51–52
  diagnostic control staff groups and, 85–87, 179, 191
  in evolution of firm, 146–147, 149, 150
  interactive control systems and, 104–105, 121, 138–139, 193
  interplay of control systems in achieving, 157, 158, 162, 169
  limited, 16–18
Audio-video conferencing, 187, 189
Automatic Data Processing (ADP), 49–51
Autonomous strategic behavior, 106–107

Bain (firm), 168
"Balanced scorecard," 68–69
Baldwin, Y. C., 54
Banking business, management control systems in, 130, 132, 140
Barnard, Chester, 40–41
Barney, J. B., 24
Barrett, M. E., 74
Bartlett, C., 191

Becker, S. W., 15
Behavior. See Human behavior
Beliefs systems, 4
  definition of, 34
  effects of information technology on, 186–189
  evolution of, in firm, 128, 134, 135–136, 148, 150, 151
  guiding strategy with, 154, 155–156, 157–158
  information and values in, 36–39
  interplay of other control systems with, 41–42, 153, 158–161, 166, 168, 173
  management responsibilities for, 55–56
  in maximizing return-on-management, 169–171
  nature of, 7–8, 10, 29, 33–36, 57–58
  summary of features of, 177, 178
Biasing, 83, 118
Birnberg, J. G., 83
BMW, 9
Boisot, M. H., 184, 185
Bonuses
  as diagnostic control incentives, 79
  in interactive control systems, 120
  to support strategic change, 137–138, 143–144, 149
  See also Incentives
Boundary systems, 4
  in controlling business conduct, 42–47
  definition of, 39
  effects of information technology on, 186, 187, 189–190
  evolution of, in firm, 128, 134–136, 148, 151

209

Boundary systems (*Continued*)
  guiding strategy with, 156, 157–158
  incentives in, 51–52
  interplay of other control systems with,
    153, 158–161, 162, 166, 168, 173,
    174
  in limiting opportunity-seeking, 39–42
  management responsibilities for, 55–56
  in maximizing return-on-management,
    169–171
  nature of, 7–8, 10, 29, 57–58
  organizational freedom and strategic do-
    mains in, 53–55
  in strategic planning, 47–51
  summary of features of, 177, 178
Branded consumer products business, man-
    agement control systems in, 130, 132,
    142
Brand revenue systems, 109, 179, 180
Brenner, S. N., 47
Breyer, J. M., 37
Brown, Donaldson, 64, 83
Brown, Wilfred, 53
Bruns, W. J., Jr., 47, 78, 183–184
Budgets
  diagnostic controls and, 61, 75, 84, 87, 179
  in evolution of control systems, 138–139,
    140, 141
  interactive controls and, 109
Burgelman, Robert, 37, 106–107
Burt, R. S., 92
Business conduct
  boundary systems for, 42–47, 51–52, 53,
    56, 179, 189
  evolution of, over firm's life cycle, 127,
    135–136, 149, 150
  See also Human behavior
Business strategy. *See* Strategy

Can manufacturing business, management
    control systems in, 130, 132, 142
Cannella, A. A., 151
Capital budgeting systems. *See* Asset acquisi-
    tion systems
Carroll, A. B., 42, 47, 52, 73
Central tendency, the paradox of, 24–26
CEO. *See* Senior management
Chandler, A. D., Jr., 91–92
Chernobyl, 55, 84, 123
Chicago Board of Trade, 43–44
Christenson, C., 40
Chrysler, 48–49
Clark, K. B., 54
Classical decision theory, 40
Codes of conduct, 42–47. *See also* Business
    conduct

Cohen, M. D., 15
Coleman, J. S., 52
Color-coded exception reporting, 187, 191
Compensation, 79–80. *See also* Incentives
Computer manufacturing business, manage-
    ment control systems in, 130, 132,
    139, 140
Computer technology. *See* Information tech-
    nology
Conduct. *See* Business conduct; Human be-
    havior
Control
  balancing empowerment and, 162–166
  definition of, 5, 60–61
  organizational nature of, 5–8
  See also Management control systems
Control staff specialists. *See* Staff specialists
Core values, 38–39, 167–168, 178, 186, 188
Critical performance variables
  analysis of, 167, 168–169
  determining, 66–72
  goal-setting to achieve, 72–75
  nature of, 63–64
  past and current use of, 64–66
  strategic uncertainties and, 94–95
  structure and communication of, 136–137,
    150, 179, 191
  See also Performance control
Cyert, Richard, 23, 92, 104–105

Daft, R. L., 15
Daniel, D. R., 64
Dearden, J., 83
Deci, E. L., 158
Dent, J. F., 57
Diagnostic control systems, 4
  alternatives to, 61–62
  asset acquisition systems as, 87–89
  comparison of interactive and, 123, 124
  in conserving management attention,
    70–71
  critical performance variables in, 63–66
  definition of, 59
  designing, 71–72
  dysfunctional side effects in, 81–84
  effects of information technology on, 186,
    187, 190–193
  empowering employees with, 165–166
  evolution of, in firm, 127–128, 136–137,
    141, 143–144, 148, 150, 151
  guiding strategy with, 156, 157–158
  implementing intended strategy in, 66–70
  incentives in, 78–81
  internal controls in, 84–85
  interplay of other control systems with,
    158–161, 173, 174

in maximizing return-on-management, 169–171

measurements and corrections in, 75–78

nature of, 7–8, 10, 29, 59–61, 89–90

staff groups in, 85–87

standards and goals in, 72–75

summary of features of, 177, 179

Diagnostic measurements, 75–78, 81

DiMaggio, P. J., 38

Doherty, V. S., 195

Donaldson, G., 55–56

Double-loop learning, 106, 160

Driver, M. J., 116

Drucker, P. E., 27

Dun & Bradstreet, 81

Dupont, 64, 90

Dyer, D., 158–160

Eastman Kodak, 16

Eccles, R. G., 78, 195

Efficiency, interplay of control systems for, 158–160

Electric utility business, management control systems in, 130, 132, 142

Electronic mail, 187, 189, 195

Emergent strategy

guiding, 154, 155–156

nature of, 20–21

Empowerment, 3, 4

balancing control and, 162–166

Evolution of control systems

allegiance to new business agenda in, 137–138

analysis of, in firm, 148–151

firm success in, 147–148

promoting strategic, 141–147

senior management in, 129–131

stages and process of, 127–129, 151–152

strategic turnaround in, 131–141

strategic uncertainties in, 138–139

Fama, E. F., 23

Feedback systems. See Diagnostic control systems

Feldman, M. S., 36, 57

Food manufacturing business, management control systems in, 130, 132, 139, 140

Ford, 80

Ford, Henry, 8

Formal control systems. See Management control systems

Franchises, codes of conduct for, 46–47

Frank, R. H., 38

Fraser, L. B., 74

Freeman, J., 134

French, J.R.P., 73

Friesen, P. H., 134

Gabarro, J. J., 133, 149

Galbraith, J. R., 94, 105

Gaming, 82–83, 118

Gatewood, R. D., 42, 52

Gellerman, S. W., 44

Geneen, Harold, 48, 52, 101, 123

General Electric, 44–45, 49, 84

General Motors, 64, 82, 90

Ghemawat, P., 16, 147

Goal-setting

in diagnostic control systems, 70, 72–75, 82, 179, 180, 190, 191

in structuring performance expectations, 136–137, 146

Goshal, S., 18

Hambrick, D. C., 151

Hannan, M. T., 134

Harvard Business School, 40

Health aids business, management control systems in, 130, 132, 140

Health care products industry, interactive control systems in, 109–110, 111

Hedberg, B., 91

Herzberg, Frederick, 22, 23

Hewlett-Packard, 9

Hierarchial strategy. See Intended strategy

Hierarchy of needs theory, 22–23

Hofstede, G., 73

Holloway, D., 55, 84, 123

Holmström, B., 23

Honda, 20

Hopwood, A. G., 73

Human behavior

boundary systems controlling, 42–44, 51–52, 53, 56

central tendency of, 24–26

control systems model of, 172–175

diagnostic systems controlling, 72–84

dynamics of, 13, 21–24

empowerment and control of, 161–166

induced and autonomous strategic, 106–107

organizational blocks in managing, 26–28, 173–174

risks in assumptions about, 171–172

Human development systems, 110

Hyundai, 9

Iacocca, Lee, 48–49

IBM

analyzing core values at, 167–168

critical performance variables and strategy at, 66–68

incentives and rewards at, 82–83

Ijiri, Y., 78
Illegal acts, 83
"Impediment to the Use of Management Information" (Mintzberg), 194–195
Incentives
  in beliefs systems, 38
  in boundary systems, 51–52
  in diagnostic control systems, 74–75, 78–81
  in evolution of control systems, 137–138, 143–144, 149, 150, 151
  in interactive control systems, 117–119
  profit planning, 119–121
  interplay of control systems fostering, 158, 160, 161, 163, 166, 174
Incremental strategy. See Emergent strategy
Induced strategic behavior, 106–107
Information codification, 184–186
Information diffusion, 184–186
Information technology
  with beliefs systems, 186, 187, 188–189
  with boundary systems, 186, 187, 189–190
  computer-based systems of, 183–184
  with diagnostic control systems, 186, 187, 190–193
  effects of, 5–8
  with interactive control systems, 186, 187, 192–195
Innovation
  interactive control systems as a catalyst for, 91–92
  interplay of control systems in fostering, 158–160, 174
  managing control systems for, 138–139, 140, 141
  opportunity and, 14–15
Input controls, 60, 61–62, 165
Intelligence systems, 109
Intended strategy
  balancing emergent strategy and, 20–21
  diagnostic controls for implementing, 63–70
  guiding, 154–155, 156
  nature of, 19–20
Interactive control systems, 4
  choosing number of, 115–117
  choosing proper, 110–114
  comparison of diagnostic and, 123, 124
  definition of, 95
  designing, 108–110
  effects of information technology on, 186, 187, 192–195
  evolution of, in firm, 128, 138–141, 148, 150, 151
  guiding strategy with, 155, 156, 157–158

incentives in, 117–119
  interplay of other control systems with, 153, 158–161, 162, 173–174
  leadership theory in, 104–105
  managers and staff groups in, 121–124
  in maximizing return-on-management, 169–171
  nature of, 7–8, 10, 29, 91–93, 95–103
  organization and systems theory in, 105–106
  profit planning as, 119–121
  psychology in, 103–104
  strategic management theory in, 106–107
  strategic planning and, 114–115
  strategic uncertainties and, 93–95
  summary of features of, 177, 180
Internal controls
  in diagnostic control systems, 84–85, 86
  summary of features of, 166, 177, 181
ITT, 48, 54, 101, 123

Jensen, Michael, 4, 23
Johnson, H. T., 64
Johnson & Johnson, 113, 118, 121
  Credo, 34, 35
Jönsson, S., 91

Kanter, R. M., 43
Kaplan, R. S., 64, 68, 78, 191
Kaufman, H., 62
Kay, E., 73
Kay, Mary, 80–81
Keller, M., 82
Kenis, I., 72
Key success factors. See Critical performance variables
Kodak, 16
Kohlberg, L., 26
Kotter, John, 17, 38, 56
Kuhn, A. J., 64

Langer, Ellen, 103–104
Lawler, E. E., III, 60, 72, 73, 76, 81, 97
Lawrence, P. R., 158–160
Leadership theory, 104–105
Learning
  double-loop, 106
  in interactive control systems, 91, 105–107, 119, 122
  interplay of control systems in fostering, 160, 161, 166, 169
  single-loop, 69, 106
Leblebici, H., 43
Levitt, T., 54
Likert, Rensis, 22
"Loose-tight controls," 161–162

Lorange, P., 18, 61, 78, 114
Lorsch, J. W., 55–56

Machinery manufacturing business, management control systems in, 130, 132, 142
Mael, F., 37
Management-by-exception
  internal controls for, 84–85
  nature of, 70–71, 90
Management-by-objectives, 171
Management control systems
  for balancing human behavior, 21–28
  for balancing opportunity and attention, 14–18
  beliefs, 33–39
  boundary, 39–55
  challenges and evaluation of, 10–11
  definition of, 5–8
  diagnostic, 59–90
  effects of information technology on, 183–195
  in firm's evolution, 141–147
  in firm's strategic turnaround, 131–141
  integration and interplay of, 153–175
  interactive, 91–124
  managers' use of, 129–131
  nature of, 3–5
  in overcoming organizational blocks, 28–29
  responsibilities in beliefs and boundary, 55–56, 57–58
  stages of, in firm, 127–129, 151–152
  strategy in, 8–10, 18–21
  success and analysis of firms using, 147–151
  summary of features of, 177–181
  See also Senior management
McDonald's, 9, 46
McGregor, Douglas, 22
McKenney, J. L., 195
McKinnon, S. M., 78, 183–184
McKinsey (firm), 168
March, James, 15, 23, 36, 57, 92, 105
Market-driven strategy, 3, 4
"Marketing Myopia" (Levitt), 54
Marriott Hotels, 46
Mary Kay Cosmetics, 80–81
Maslow, Abraham, 22–23
MasterCard, 49
Mayo, Elton, 22
Measures, properties of, 76–78
Meckling, W. H., 23
Merchant, K., A., 11, 43, 47, 61, 74–75, 79, 161
Meyer, H. H., 73

Meyer, J. W., 38
Middle management, 121–122. See also Senior management
Mihalek, P. H., 47
Miller, D., 134
Mindfulness, 103–104
Mindlessness, 103–104
Mintzberg, Henry, 8–9, 10, 17, 19, 21, 59, 115, 154, 194–195
Mission statements, 128, 134–135, 150, 178
Molander, E. A., 47
Motivation. See Goal-setting; Incentives
Murray, P. J., 47

Nelson, R. R., 40, 134
Newman, W. H., 134
Nike, 9
Nohria, N., 195
Nonaka, Ikujiro, 37, 122
Nordstrom, 46–47, 64, 66
Norton, D. P., 68, 78, 191

Olsen, J. P., 15
Open-ended goals, 73
Opportunity
  balancing attention and, 16–18
  controlling search for, 33, 58
    in beliefs systems, 37–38
    in boundary systems, 39, 47–51, 54–55
    in diagnostic control systems, 70
    in interactive control systems, 99–103
  creating, 14–16, 40, 158
  interplay of control systems for, 156, 157, 158, 162, 164
  unlimited, 17–18
Opportunity space
  definition of, 16
  effects of beliefs systems and boundary systems on, 37–38, 41–42, 58
  using control levers to manage, 153–158
  See also Opportunity
Organizational blocks, 26–28, 173–174
Organization and systems theory, 105–106
Organizations
  balancing opportunity and attention in, 14–18
  controlling business strategy in, 28–29
  dynamics and nature of, 13, 29–30
  human motives in, 21–28
  overcoming inertia in, 133–136
  strategy making in, 18–21
  using management control systems to test, 145–146
  See also Management control systems
Ouchi, W. G., 24, 59

Output controls
    alternatives to diagnostic control systems,
        61–62
    nature of, 59–60

Paper manufacturing business, management
        control systems in, 130, 132, 142
Pascale, R. T., 20
Pepsi, 47, 94, 96, 97, 98–99
Performance control
    diagnostic systems and, 59–60
    evolution of management systems in, 136–
        137, 142–144, 146
    See also Critical performance variables
Perrow, C., 43, 53, 54
Peters, T. J., 161
Porter, M. E., 16, 54, 91, 147
Post-audit, 88–89
Powell, W. W., 38
Principles of Scientific Management (Taylor),
        21–22
Process engineering, 164–165
Professional Conduct Committee of the Insti-
        tute of Chartered Accountants of On-
        tario, 46
Profit planning systems
    diagnostic, 61
    in evolution of management control sys-
        tems, 138–139, 140
    interactive, 109, 113, 119–121, 180, 193
Project management systems, 109, 113, 114
Promotions, 119. See also Incentives
Psychology, interactive control systems and,
        103–104

Quinn, J. B., 151

"Rabble hypothesis," 22, 23
Rathe, A. W., 5
Realized strategy, 154–156
Results control, 59–60
Retail manufacturer and merchant business,
        management control systems in, 130,
        132, 142
Return-on-investment (ROI), 17, 51, 64, 65,
        83
Return-on-management (ROM)
    interrelation of control systems and, 158,
        169–171
    maximizing, 17–18, 70
Rewards. See Incentives
Rhode, J. G., 60, 72, 76, 97
Riccardo, John, 48
Rich, A. J., 47

Risks
    analyzing and avoiding strategic, 48–51,
        167, 168
    in assumptions about human behavior,
        171–172
Roberts, J., 42
Romanelli, E., 134
Rowan, B., 38
Roy Rogers Restaurants, 47
Ryan, R. M., 158

Salancik, G. R., 43
Salaries, 137–138
Salomon Brothers, 45
Sanctions, 52. See also Business conduct
Scapens, R., 42
Schön, D., 55, 69
Schroder, H. M., 116
Scott Morton, M. S., 18, 61, 78
Sculley, John, 96, 97, 98–99, 100
Sears, 16, 81
Self-interest, 22–25, 171–173
Selznick, P., 57–58
Senge, P. M., 151
Senior management
    in analyzing strategic variables, 166–169
    in balancing empowerment and control,
        161–166
    in beliefs and boundary systems, 55–56,
        57–58
    in diagnostic control systems, 70–71,
        85–87
    in firm's evolution, 141–147
    in firm's strategic turnaround, 131–133
    in gaining allegiance to new agenda,
        137–138
    informational needs of, 5–8
    in interactive control systems, 91–93, 95–
        107, 121–124
    in maximizing return-on-management,
        169–171
    in overcoming organizational blocks, 28–29
    in overcoming organizational inertia,
        133–136
    in realizing human potential, 171–175
    in revising strategy and control systems,
        139–141
    strategic uncertainties for, 93–95, 138–139
    in structuring performance expectations,
        136–137
    success and analysis of, 147–151
    summary of control functions of, 170,
        177–181
    use of control systems by, 129–131
    See also Management control systems

Siers, H. L., 52, 56
Simon, Herbert, 16, 17
Simons, R., 11, 49, 56, 66, 68, 84, 94, 96, 100, 101, 109, 113, 117, 122, 191
Single-learning loop, 69, 106, 160
Sloan, Alfred, 107
Smith, C. S., 47
Smoothing, 83
Staff specialists
  in beliefs and boundary systems, 56–57
  in diagnostic control systems, 85–87
  in interactive control systems, 121–124
  in maximizing return-on-management, 169–171
  summary of duties of, 170, 178, 179, 180, 181
Standardization
  creativity and, 61–62
  empowerment and, 164–165
"Standards of Ethical Conduct for Management Accountants" (Institute of Management Accountants), 46
Stedry, A., 73
Steiner, G. A., 114
Strategic management theory, 106–107
Strategic planning
  boundary systems for, 47–51
  education in evolution of, 144–146
  interactive systems and, 114–115, 116
  interplay of control systems in, 171, 179
Strategic uncertainties
  analyzing, 167, 169
  focusing attention on, 138–139, 146–147, 193
  nature of, 93–95
Strategy
  in achieving return-on-management, 169–171
  analysis of variables in, 166–169
  balancing intended and emergent, 20–21
  boundary systems for, 47–51, 53–55
  of controlling organizational blocks, 28–29
  control systems in evolution of, 141–147
  control systems in redirecting, 131–141
  definition and nature of, 8–10, 153–158
  dynamics of making, 13, 18–20, 158–161
  interactive controls systems and, 93–95, 114–115, 116–117
  in realizing human potential, 171–175
  of tight versus loose control, 161–166
Streufert, S., 116
Subjective rewards, 117–119
Sweeney, R. B., 52, 56

Taylor, Frederick, 21–22, 62
Taylor, W., 92
Technology. See Information technology
Tightness of controls
  balancing empowerment and, 162–166
  nature of, 161–162
Tiryakian, E. A., 11
Top management. See Senior management
Tosi, H., 73
Total quality systems, 171
Trice, H. M., 37
Turiel, E., 26
Turner Construction Company, 100–101, 118, 121, 122
Turopolec, L., 83
Tushman, M. L., 134

Umapathy, S., 61, 83
USA Today, 100, 169

Value
  dynamics of creating, 13, 14–18
  interplay of control systems in achieving, 157, 158, 164, 166, 167–168, 173
  See also Core values
Value chains, 112, 120
Video conferencing, 187, 189
VISA, 49
Vogel, John, 52

Wal-Mart, 16, 46
Wang Computer, 54
Warren, D. L., 136
Waterman, R. H., 161
Watson, Thomas J., Jr., 167
Weissinger–Baylon, R., 15
Welch, John, Jr., 49
Western Electric Company, 20
Westley, F. R., 37
Weston, H., 49, 66, 68, 100, 101, 122
White, Harrison, 79–80
Williamson, O. E., 80
Winter, S. G., 40, 134
Workouts, 164–165
Work standards, empowerment and, 164–165

Yin, T., 81
Young, S. M., 83

Zack, M. H., 195
Zero-based budgeting, 171
Zuboff, S., 191

About the Author

Robert Simons is a professor of business administration at Harvard Business School. During the last eleven years, Simons has taught accounting, strategy, and management control courses in both the Harvard MBA Program and the Executive Education Programs. A Canadian Chartered Accountant, Simons worked as an auditor and consultant with Price Waterhouse before earning his Ph.D. from McGill University with a joint concentration in control and business policy.

His ongoing research into the relationship between business strategy and management control systems has been published in academic journals and books such as *Strategic Management Journal*, *Accounting, Organizations and Society*, *Contemporary Accounting Research*, *Accounting and Management: Field Study Perspectives*, and *Journal of Accounting Literature*.

Professor Simons has served as a consultant to a number of corporations on matters of organization structure, strategic planning, and control systems. He has testified as an expert witness before State Public Utility Commissions and in U.S. Federal Court. He lives with his wife and three children in Cohasset, twenty miles south of Boston.

217